WILLS, PROBATE, and REAL ESTATE

What You Don't Know Can Cost You Thousands

A Comprehensive Blueprint for
Estate Preparation and Administration

SANDRA BRAZELTON
and
ALEXANDRIA BRAZELTON

TESTIMONIALS

"A Must Read for All Families"
Betty Marshall, MBA – Retired City-Clerk Treasurer

"Wills, Probate, and Real Estate is an excellent, "How to" book that details the process, along with the issues and pitfalls of probate that are faced by all who have lost loved ones.

Its detailed checklists and worksheets make what is considered a dreaded process, an easier task.

After stumbling through this process in the past, I easily recommend this book as a must-read for all families."

Chanda Crutcher
CEO of American Senior Assistance Programs (ASAP)
"I'm believing that the impact of this effort on our community will be significant!
Thank you for being such a community trail blazer!
Lives will be better because of this."

Floyd Rodgers, Evangelist
"Insightful and informative. Your knowledge, vision, motivation, and concern for others will bless many."

Jerry A. Mitchell, President/CEO
Alabama State Black Chamber of Commerce (ASBCC
"Comprehensive and insightful. This blueprint goes over and above the basic information that I have seen most clients receive."

DEDICATION

"For *I know the plans I have for you*," declares the LORD, "*plans* to prosper *you* and not to harm *you, plans* to give *you* hope and a future." ... Jeremiah 29:11

This book is dedicated to the hardworking families and entrepreneurs who are committed to the Universal principles of generational wealth. Your vision to work as hard to protect your wealth as you have to develop it will provide a powerful legacy.

ACKNOWLEDGEMENTS

It Takes a Village

This book represents years of experience, time, study, resources, courage, and application.

When we shared our vision and sent out excerpts to our influencers, support groups, and contributors, the response was overwhelming.

This book immediately connected to their experiences, fears, frustrations, and goals as servant leaders.

They understand this is a movement to lead a mindset shift through education, empowerment, support, and action.

I would like to thank God for His infinite intellect, unlimited capacity, and for giving us the vision, courage, and ability to create this unique document.

I would like to thank my family for their unconditional love and support.

My daughter and co-author, Alexandria Brazelton, thank you for choosing to carry the torch of generational wealth for our family. I love you and I am so blessed by your work ethic, integrity, and tenacity.

Editor

Our editor, Jessica Ragland, is our secret weapon.

Jessica, you are brilliant, thorough, talented, gifted, supportive, and encouraging.

Thank you for taking this fantastic journey with me.

Publisher

Thank you, Suzanne Doyle-Ingram with Prominence Publishing.

Your guidance and expertise will help this reach the masses in a serious, professional, and compelling manner.

Contributors

Our powerful contributors have made this book rich, diverse, and highly relevant by the insights they provide from their areas of subject matter expertise.

Law

Scott Rogers, Attorney - Secure Law Firm

Michael Adams, Vice-President - Secure Title

Thank you for always going above and beyond to provide the guidance, support, protection, and grounding we need.

Clergy

Floyd Rodgers, Evangelist - Blue Spring Road Church of Christ

You are a phenomenal man of God and powerful servant leader.

We are blessed to have you as our minister.

Business

Jerry A. Mitchell, President/CEO - Alabama State Black Chamber of Commerce (ASBCC)

Jerry, your support through the years has been invaluable. Thank you for your self-less leadership and commitment to business excellence and equality.

Finance

Ken Battles, Founder/President - Compass Urban Stewardship Ministries

You are brilliant and your servant leadership is inspiring. I have always leaned on you and you always come through as my brother and my advisor.

Geriatrics

Chanda Crutcher, CEO - American Senior Assistance Programs (ASAP)

Your passion, expertise, and labor of love in this area is unsurpassed.

We are all blessed through your gifts.

Business

Betty Marshall, MBA - Retired City Clerk Treasurer

I am inspired by your intellect and humbled by your support.

Thank you for your thorough and heartfelt contribution.

FOREWORD

Wills, Probate, and Real Estate is dedicated to hard working families and entrepreneurs who are committed to the Universal principles of generational wealth.

As children of God, real estate brokers, real estate instructors, and business advisors, it breaks my heart to see how we waste our inheritance through miseducation, ignorance, and lack of action.

Death is an emotionally fragile time for Personal Representatives and their families. There are legal guidelines, emotions, and a lot of work involved in estate administration.

Most administrators have never gone through probate so much of the anxiety comes from not knowing what to ask and not knowing what to expect.

Plus, many of them do not have the information, support, or game plan that they need to protect the estate.

Over the past 30 years, we have found that there is a lot of miseducation in regards to how real estate is handled in probating an estate. In addition, most real estate agents are not experienced in this sensitive area. Therefore, this book bridges the gap and guides the reader through the maze of probate to ensure success from a real estate perspective.

Also, most information on this subject comes from attorneys.

However, we are real estate brokers and we chose to write this book because real estate is usually the largest asset of an estate so the need for our professional guidance in this area is critical.

This book includes specific strategies to protect generational wealth, specifically as it relates to real estate.

Our clients trust our expertise and experience to provide them guidance and solutions that help them avoid the financial pitfalls and loss of real estate as a result of improper probate education, preparation, and execution.

In addition, we provide a real world perspective with actual examples from the field because we work directly with the family members who trust us to help guide them through this unfamiliar territory.

This book will prepare you for the inevitability of death so you can have the tools, strategies, knowledge, confidence, and resources to direct your assets to your intended heirs, charities, and ministries of your choice.

CONTENTS

INTRODUCTION

Millions and millions of dollars are sucked from estates that are not properly structured and executed. In fact, according to the American Association of Retired Persons (AARP), six in ten adults that die do not have a Will.

Many of the decedents endured tremendous hardship and sacrifice to be able to provide the generational wealth to their children, charity, and legacy. However, by neglecting to protect their assets through proper estate planning, often times the entire inheritance is wasted or surrendered back to the state and the care of their minor children is left up for grabs.

Over the past 30 years as real estate brokers, real estate probate specialists, business advisors, real estate investors, and real estate instructors, we have seen first-hand how unprepared families waste a lot of the estate assets, lose the property, lose the business, and endure years of stress, family discourse, and legal liability.

These first-hand experiences represent our motivation for developing this book as our gift to generational wealth.

Also, real estate is usually the largest estate asset in an estate and most real estate agents are not trained in probate real estate. In addition, the estate attorney may need professional real estate information to help the Executor receive proper guidance and representation.

Therefore, this book is a resource, wake-up call, road map, and plea for action for families, executors, entrepreneurs, child care services, probate administrators, businesses, attorneys, clergy, health care professionals, funeral home administrators, geriatric professionals, insurance agents, real estate professionals, and all those that support families before, during, and after the loss of a loved one.

CHAPTER 1

Blueprint Goals and Objectives

The goal of this blueprint is to use our 30 years of experience and top 1% nationwide credentials to provide you with a road map beginning with entering probate and ending with the successful sale of real estate and the disposition of assets that are included in the estate.

There are two major sections of this blueprint:

Section 1 will provide detailed checklists, recommendations, and strategies that you can implement immediately when you serve as Executor/Personal Representative.

If you are currently involved in probate, the 50 Point Checklist to Follow After Notification of Death will help you understand what to expect so you can make informed decisions and succeed as the Executor of this important position.

This is also a powerful training guide to share with others so they can better understand your responsibilities, educate themselves, and provide valuable support during this tender time.

Section 2 of this blueprint is a comprehensive planning guide that provides worksheets to cover many of the critical areas of estate planning.

If you are not currently in probate, and even if you do not have a Will, this information and the strategies within will better prepare you to avoid many of the financial pitfalls associated with improper probate preparation and administration.

This section also provides information on preparing a Will, Durable Power of Attorney, Living Will, and a Health Care Directive provided by Attorney Scott A. Rogers of Secure Law, PC in Huntsville, Alabama. This information will be invaluable when you meet with your estate attorney to execute these critical documents.

There are also over 40 worksheets to help you identify family members, assets, liabilities, and estate management strategies to complete your Estate Planning Workbook.

Most importantly, regardless of your probate status, this blueprint will be your road map to support, educate, and empower yourself and others so you can protect generational wealth.

These are the five objectives of this blueprint:

1. Help Personal Representatives Avoid the Financial Pitfalls of Probate
2. Provide Inside Secrets to Prepare Executors to Settle the Real Estate Involved in Probate
3. Provide Risk Mitigation Strategies to Save Time, Money, and Stress
4. Unravel Many of the Myths Associated with Probate Requirements
5. Empower Executives with Tools and Resources to Prepare and Succeed in Probate and to Protect Generational Wealth

After completion of this book, you will have a personalized and detailed document that will provide specific instructions for your family, executor, doctors, attorneys, and all those involved in honoring your last wishes. We are honored to use our top 1% nationwide credentials and probate experience to serve you during this sensitive and critical time.

CHAPTER 2

Basic Estate Planning Documents

Estate planning is a complex area of law that is tied to your goals and assets. That is why you should use an experienced estate attorney. This book covers basic estate planning. These are the four basic documents that we will discuss.

Last Will and Testament, Durable Power of Attorney, Living Will, and Health Care Proxy

We have templates and actual copies for each of these in the book which were provided by the law office of local attorney Scott Rogers. These templates make it easy for you to fill in the information and have it verified and properly executed by an estate attorney for accuracy.

Last Will and Testament

So why do you need a Will? This is a very interesting question so let me answer it with a question.

How many of you have children, grandchildren, nieces and nephews that you love?

If their parents or guardian die Without a Will, would you want the placement of these children left up to the courts?

Historically, many of us understand the atrocities of separation of families, but this one is avoidable through proactive preparation and action.

How many of you have parents, aunts, uncles, grandparents, siblings, and other immediate family? Where is their insurance policy, how would they like to be buried or remembered?

It takes courage and leadership to ask these hard questions but the consequences and tremendous loss of generational wealth should motivate you. This should be the topic of family dinners, sorority and fraternity meetings, family reunions, non-profits, etc.

In fact, the workbook section has over 40 worksheets to help you start this conversation and to document this critical information in an organized and responsible manner.

What about you, someone is going to have to make these decisions on your behalf. The purpose of estate planning is to clean up your mess.

If you inherited some property or assets, what person or entity would you want to bless?

Are you going to leave your loved ones hanging out or prepared?

You should want your legacy in death to be as responsible as your legacy in life.

Plus, it's not just about you. You stand on the shoulder of those before you who endured tremendous hardship and sacrifice to be able to provide the generational wealth to their children, charity, and legacy.

Some of them did not know better, but after today, you will be without excuse so the best thing you can do to honor them is to provide clear choices and leadership for your heirs to follow in a proactive and responsible manner

There are some situations where an attorney may determine that the probate process is not necessary. This usually occurs for example, when there are absolutely no assets in the name of the decedent, no creditors or predators, or the estate is being distributed through trusts, property deeds, contractual payable on death beneficiaries, etc.

Durable Power of Attorney

This document needs to be executed immediately, whether you have a Will or not.

A Durable Power of Attorney is the document used to name a person whom you trust to make decisions for yourself or your estate in the event you become unable to do so. If you have a medical emergency without this documentation, it may require expensive and time consuming court intervention to execute your business.

Living Will

A Living Will is a document that states that in the event that you are declared, by two qualified physicians, to have a terminal condition with no hope of recovery and can only remain alive through the use of life support systems, whether or not you wish your death to be prolonged by the life support systems. If this situation occurs and you do not have a Living Will, your family will make the decision for you. Hospitals generally will ask you or your family, upon arrival, if you have a Living Will.

This is an important decision, so please consider it carefully.

<u>Health Care Proxy</u>

This is the person you designate to provide health care instructions on your behalf if you are no longer able to do it. There are templates and actual documents in the book so this will save you a lot time and stress

Leaving an inheritance is a spiritual mandate. There are many types of inheritances such as work ethic and integrity but this inheritance specifically relates to wealth.

Proverbs 13:22 says a good man or woman leaves an inheritance. How many of you are good men and women? To me this implies that a bad man or woman does not leave an inheritance. When I experience this indifferent attitude, I pray for those individuals because "to him that knows to do good and doeth it not, to him it is sin." James 4:17

In fact, I had a close family member who refused estate planning. Her attitude was just let them fight over it. That is really a shackled and selfish mindset because death should be a celebration of your life. However, if you intentionally neglect your affairs, your legacy will be tainted and your influence will be weakened. Preparation is also a spiritual mandate. You don't want to leave others burdened with these major and emotional decisions during a crisis so please make the decision to be proactive, do the work now, take the high road and trust the blessings of leaving an inheritance by fulfilling this mandates.

Lack of Will Preparation Is a Common Problem

It is very rewarding to see the family members, beneficiaries, churches, non-profits, business owners, etc. receive their intended benefits when a loved one passes away.

These funds can be used to pay off debt, save money, finish college, purchase a home, strengthen financial resources, and to support missions and ministries that are near and dear to the decedent.

However, the list of those who die intestate, (without a Will) covers all ages, races, backgrounds, and professions. It ranges from Presidents to lawyers to entrepreneurs, athletes, musicians, and everything in between.

According to USA Today.com and Legalzoom.com, Abraham Lincoln was the 16th President and a lawyer who died without a Will.

The article also states it took 34 years to settle the estate of billionaire entrepreneur, Howard

Hughes.

It is reported that International musician Bob Marley knew he had lung cancer that lingered for several months, but he did not have a Will so his estate had dozens of claimants.

National Football League (NFL) professional quarterback, Steve McNair, looked successful from the outside, but he was allegedly shot by his girlfriend and he did not have a Will to protect his family.

Aretha Franklin, Prince, and Congressman Sonny Bono are reported to have died intestate and lost millions from their estate in legal costs and claims.

CHAPTER 3

Real Estate Agents and Probate

Real estate is the largest lifetime investment for most families.

However, when real estate becomes a part of an estate due to the death of a loved one, it adds additional stress, financial and legal pressure to the already overwhelming responsibilities of the Personal Representative.

When there is real estate involved in the probate process, the transaction must be handled differently than a traditional real estate transaction.

We are experienced real estate brokers that specialize in probate real estate so we understand the specific strategies and documentation that apply to probate estates that contain real estate.

We have found that just as attorneys have different levels of specialization, most real estate agents' specializations vary as well and often do not include real estate probate.

However, since real estate is usually the most valuable asset in an estate, our clients trust us to use our skills and experience to support them and to help them succeed through the maze of probate during this crucial time.

Also, an experienced estate attorney can help you with advanced strategies to avoid the time, expense, and exposure of probate by using trusts, gifting, joint ownership, payable on death registration, etc.

However, this blueprint will help you accomplish the basics of estate planning documentation so you are prepared if there is an emergency before you pursue advanced estate planning options.

CHAPTER 4

15 Step Executor Checklist for Probate with Real Estate

Please follow this check list to protect the real estate as you go through probate.

	Real Estate Information
1	Obtain and Review Property Deeds
2	Obtain Pay Off Amounts of All Mortgages, Including Home Equity Lines of Credit
3	Make Mortgage Payments
4	Pay Property Taxes
5	Pay Home Owners Insurance
6	Pay Home Owner Association (HOA) Fees
7	Check Home Warranties
8	Check Lawn Maintenance
9	Check Escrow Account
10	Check for Mortgage Insurance
11	Choose Real Estate Agent
12	Obtain Title Search on Property and Decedent to Check for Unknown Liens and Mortgages
13	Develop Marketing Strategy ("As Is", Investor, Traditional, Etc.)
14	Determine Value Based on Marketing Strategy
15	Pay for All Property Repairs to Avoid Mechanics Liens

CHAPTER 5

6 Money Sucking Probate Real Estate Threats

Part of probate success is having the knowledge and information you need ahead of time so you are proactive instead of reactive.

By knowing what to look for and what to look out for in advance, you can avoid a lot of the stress, anxiety, time, and expense of probate.

As previously stated, the Executor is the most important person because he/she will be responsible for executing your wishes.

Therefore, it is wise and important to ensure that the Executor is informed and prepared in advance.

The Executor has both short term and long term responsibilities.

Immediately after notification of death, the Executor will need access to funds and information to cover burial costs and estate expenses until probate is resolved.

The easiest way to prepare for this is to add the Executor as the contingent beneficiary on active financial accounts such as checking, saving, and brokerage accounts.

The Executor is also responsible for paying the bills of the estate until probate is closed.

This is a very vulnerable time for the Executor and the estate.

In many situations, there are not enough immediate funds available to handle short term expenses.

The deadliest real estate threats to the estate are lack of professional guidance from trained probate real estate specialists to determine accurate property value, mortgage payments, home owner insurance, property taxes, home owner association (HOA) liens, and mechanic liens.

1. Lack of Professional Guidance from Trained Probate Real Estate Specialists to Determine Accurate Property Value

We are hemorrhaging generational wealth at the expense of the blood, sweat, tears, and sacrifices of those who came before us. We see many situations where farm land is now expensive commercial development, high rise housing, etc. Real estate prices and demand change continually and without proper, current information you may be giving away your hard earned inheritance. Please reach out to us immediately if you have any heir property or if you know of anyone who has heir property so we can help determine the highest and best use of the property and the best current value. Do not allow fast talk and quick money to rob you of generational wealth.

2. Mortgage Payment Threat

Many estates go into foreclosure during probate because the mortgage is not paid. The Executor must be proactive to ensure that all mortgage payments are current. This is especially important if there has been a long-term illness.

Remember to check on the status of home equity lines of credit and reverse mortgages. Also, check the escrow balance to ensure sufficient funds are available for home owner insurance, property taxes, etc.

3. Home Owner Insurance Threat

Do not assume that the home owner insurance is paid even if the home has a mortgage. Typically, federally insured mortgages such as VA and FHA require the home owner insurance to be included in the payment. However, there are many non-traditional mortgage loans that require the insurance to be paid separately. Also, if there is no mortgage on the home, the insurance is paid separately. If the home owner insurance is not paid, the estate is at risk for loss due to fire, theft, natural disaster, etc. Please do not risk the entire estate by neglecting this critical area.

4. Property Tax Threat

We have personally witnessed a massive amount of wealth forfeited due to lack of property tax payment. It is imperative that the Executor ensure that property taxes are current. Some counties issue annual tax statements and some have public websites. Also, the mortgage statement may show if there are taxes and insurance being paid monthly through escrow accounts.

In most states, whoever pays the property taxes has an interest in the property. Municipalities administer property tax sales so it can have the revenue to meet its obligations and they do not care who pays the property taxes.

The worst thing that can happen is for the estate to undergo additional legal expense due to a tax lien or even worse, lose the property.

The tax lien owner has legal rights to the property and a civil proceeding is usually required to resolve this.

Many investors are very savvy in this area and there are tax lien classes that teach others how to acquire, control, and cash flow properties using tax liens.

They also learn how to pursue quiet title strategies to become the legal owner.

We have personally been involved with a property that the tax sale owner would lease to families with lease provisions that do not guarantee the term of the lease and place the families at risk.

The owner of the tax lien intentionally ignored all certified mail requests from the deeded owner because he did not want payment for the tax lien. His business model was to use the non-refundable money from leasing the tax sale property over and over again to vulnerable families.

These tenants did not understand what was going on because they were receiving letters to the property from the mortgage company regarding property foreclosure while paying rent to the tax lien holder.

When this situation was legally investigated, we were told it was a civil matter because the tax lien holder had a legal interest in the property.

In fact, we have a property in our neighborhood right now that has been neglected for twenty years because it is entangled in a tax lien. Please do not let this happen to your heir property.

5. Home Owner Association (HOA) Lien Threat

Unpaid HOA fees can result in property liens. Sometimes these are paid through the mortgage. However, please be proactive and ensure they are paid.

6. Mechanic Lien Threat

Mechanic liens can be filed for unpaid repairs. Most states allow a statutory timeline for them to be filed so be aware of any recent repairs and make sure you obtain proof of payment.

CHAPTER 6

10 Executor Strategies to Immediately Protect the Estate

Many of the pitfalls of probate can be avoided by awareness, preparation, and action.

This is a list of 10 short term strategies that will help your Executor succeed while the probate process continues:

You will find the worksheets to record this information in Section 2 of this blueprint.

1. Consider setting up automatic payments for all bills and debts. Also, sign up for overdraft protection on the bill payment account. This will ensure that critical services such as mortgage payments, utilities, etc. are not interrupted.

2. Add signature authority and contingent beneficiary status for the Executor on active, financial accounts such as checking, saving, and brokerage accounts. This will allow the Executor immediate access to funds.

3. Place key information in a safe deposit box or other fire proof and secure location. Remember, if you use a safe deposit box, make sure your Executor or someone you trust is listed on the account and make sure they have a key and know the location.

4. Make sure the Executor has a key to your home, business, and vehicle.

5. Make sure the Executor has access to all alarm codes for home, business, car, etc. Remember to also provide the verbal alarm code so the Executor will be prepared if the alarm company calls.

6. Make sure Executor has the password for your mobile phone, laptop, etc.

7. Make sure your Executor has a valid copy of your Will and any Codicils.

8. Make sure your Executor has a contact list for beneficiaries.

9. Make sure your Executor has immediate access to life insurance policies, brokerage accounts, bank accounts, and any other financial documents.

10 Make sure your Executor has access to online accounts with user name and password.

This checklist will provide peace of mind because it will ensure that all critical services will continue without disruption or additional fees while the estate is being settled.

CHAPTER 7

Our Real Estate Probate Services

As your full-service, probate real estate experts, we specialize in listing and selling properties in probate.

Based on our 30 years of experience, we realize there is no "one-size fits all solution" to dispose of real estate. For example, you may decide to liquidate the property "As Is" with our quick cash investor service or through a traditional listing. Our goal is to work with you to develop the best solution.

Also, regardless of where the property is located, we can help you with the real estate transaction.

We have cash investors, buyers, reputable contacts, local service providers, and referral services that can handle all aspects of probate properties.

You can trust us to help you through this sensitive moment in time because we know what to do, how to do it, and when to do it.

Our goal is to support you and to professionally and respectfully address your questions and concerns.

This blueprint contains information that specifically applies to real estate in probate.

For example, in addition to our Satisfied Seller 25 Step Checklist that we use as part of our traditional listing success strategy, we also developed 25 Inside Secrets to Avoid Real Estate Probate Financial Disaster.

This is a summary of the 25 activities we perform on your behalf using our professional, top 1% expertise to list and sell your home:

Satisfied Seller 25 Step Checklist

1	View Property
2	Listen to Understand Seller Goals and Priorities
3	Gather Relevant Comparables
4	Analyze Comparables
5	Review data and develop a listing strategy based on seller goals and comparables
6	Prepare Seller Estimate Proceeds
	Obtain pay off amounts, verify signers, power of attorney, trust, etc.
7	Execute listing agreement
	Execute legally required seller documentation to ensure compliance with Alabama Law
8	Make Recommendations to Prepare Home for Market based on Seller Goals
9	Manage Marketing Plan: Manage Pictures Manage Signage Manage Technology Manage Video Manage Social Media Manage Flyers Manage Lockbox access and keys Manage MLS Use Marketing Expertise to Market Home to Attract Agents and Buyers
10	Manage and Coordinate Showings with agents, buyers, and investors
11	Show Property as requested
12	Use professional skills to answer questions

1 3	Receive Offers
1 4	Use professional skills to evaluate offer
1 5	Use professional skills to negotiate offer
1 6	Manage Offer Sales Contract Inspection Addendum Request for Repairs, etc. Counter Offer Addendum
1 7	Manage Buyer Manage buyer qualification Manage and monitor buying process - lender, title, underwriter, appraisal, insurance, clear to close, etc. Verifications of employment, rental, banking deposit, taxes, liens, etc.
1 8	Coordinate inspections: Termite Home Inspection Radon Inspection, etc. Energy, Roof, Septic, etc. Lead based paint
1 9	Evaluate and Manage Inspection Results
2 0	Follow up on Repairs and execute documentation to keep contract current
2 1	Follow up on appraisal, loan status, repair status, etc.
2 2	Review Closing Documents
2 3	Manage Closing Process Coordinate closing time and logistics Review Settlement Statement with Seller
2 4	Coordinate Final Walkthrough, etc.

2 5	Attend Closing

In addition to the traditional listing duties, we want to prepare, educate, and support the Personal Representative/Executor/Administrator through the specialized maze of the real estate part of the probate process.

CHAPTER 8

25 Inside Secrets to Avoid Real Estate Probate Financial Disaster

As the Personal Representative, one of your responsibilities is to evaluate and protect the assets of the estate. This checklist will provide awareness and guidance to help you protect the real estate as you move through probate.

1. Choose an Experienced Probate Real Estate Professional
2. Choose an Experienced Probate Real Estate Attorney
3. Obtain a Title Search on the property and the Decedent to uncover unexpected property liens and creditor
4. Obtain a Credit Report on the Decedent to uncover unknown creditors
5. Secure a list of personal property
6. Secure date and time stamped pictures and videos of all personal property including vehicles
7. Remove all valuables from the property
8. Remove any safety hazards such as firearms, etc. from the property
9. Remove personal property from the house, garage, sheds, etc. as soon as possible. Consider using air controlled storage facilities to protect contents
10. Remove clutter from the house
11. Make sure the house is clean and smells fresh

12. Maintain Access to a Notary to facilitate the execution of legal documents
13. Maintain Home Owner Insurance on the Property to protect it from losses until it is sold
14. Check property consistently for unexpected repair problems, vandalism, etc.
15. Keep utilities on to keep the pipes from freezing
16. Turn the water off at the meter and winterize the home prevent pipes from freezing
17. Keep the yard maintained
18. Exchange contact information with neighbors and ask them to contact you if they see any one accessing the property
19. Keep copies of all documentation signed and stored on the cloud for quick access
20. Secure the property and change the locks
21. Keep separate records and account of all estate expenses
22. Check and/or forward the mail
23. Keep all beneficiaries updated with consistent and transparent communication
24. Stay abreast of and comply with all legal timelines
25. Pay all estate bills and keep receipts

CHAPTER 9

The Personal Representative, Executor/Administrator, and Real Estate

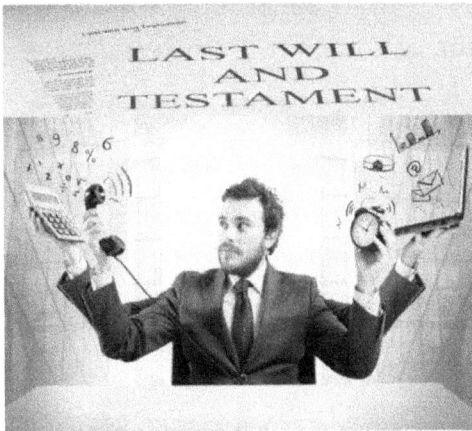

The most important person in the probate process is the Executor.

The Executor is also called the Personal Representative and/or Administrator.

This is an honorable position of trust and service. However, in addition to everything the Executor may have going on and the grief he or she may be experiencing, the Executor has to efficiently and ethically unravel a lifetime of property, investments, liabilities, wishes, and other concerns of the deceased all while being held accountable by family and the court system. The Administrator often has no probate experience and without a Will, there may not be any information.

Plus, there may not be immediate access to funds to pay the current bills and to protect the estate.

It is understandable if you are feeling overwhelmed right now because handling real estate is just one small part of all of your duties and responsibilities as Executor or Administrator.

Over the past 30 years, our company has been honored to help many families and entities successfully liquidate the real estate that is part of estates in probate.

The owners of the real estate worked hard to provide and secure the financial legacy that they wanted to share with their chosen beneficiaries.

Therefore, if you are the Personal Representative/Administrator/ Executor, it is important for you to remember that although you may have detailed knowledge and expertise in many areas, the probate process is different and you need professional guidance, especially when real estate is involved.

One of the challenges we see is that those who take a "Do-it-Yourself (DIY)" approach to this very serious responsibility often do so without proper knowledge because most Personal Representatives have never gone through probate.

We have worked with Executors who would not seek or follow professional guidance so they end up wasting thousands of dollars of the estate and enduring years of unnecessary and avoidable time, stress, and expenses in probate. As a result, estate assets that could be directed to the beneficiaries were wasted. In addition, they forfeit generational wealth by taking the first offer without current real estate value information from trained real estate probate experts.

Seven Benefits of Estate Planning

Documenting and protecting your estate provides peace of mind and honors your worth in a very responsible and noble manner.

1. It Saves Your Estate Thousands of Dollars
2. It Prevents Unnecessary and Expensive Delays
3. It Reduces Family Stress and Anxiety
4. It Allows You to Choose the Guardian of Your Dependents/Minor Children
5. It Provides Emotional Support and Security to Your Personal Representative/ Executor and Family Because They Do Not Have to Guess About What You Want
6. It Allows You to Designate Your Chosen Beneficiaries
7. It Protects Your Estate from Predators and Others Who May Choose to Claim an Interest in Your Estate

Choosing an Executor

This decision should be made prayerfully, carefully, and wisely.

In addition to the ten attributes listed below, think about the maturity, wealth mindset, and experience of your choice for both your primary and alternate executor.

Think about the income level, discernment, experience, ethics, and wisdom of your choice.

The wrong Executor can bankrupt an estate willfully or through improper execution due to lack of knowledge and understanding of the process and through bad decisions.

We personally, would not leave an estate with multiple real estate holdings to an Executor who does not own real estate or other assets and who has not exercised sound financial wisdom and judgment over his/her own assets.

Also, if you are leaving money in trust for your dependents, consider distributing it in phases at different ages. In some cases, a one lump sum payment may be too tempting but a phased distribution may provide valuable time and life experience to mold the maturity and judgment of the beneficiary.

There are many horror stories of heirs who are wealthy in their twenties due to an inheritance and broke three years later.

Please consider these 10 attributes when choosing your Personal Representative/Executor:

10 Attributes of a Good Probate Personal Representative/Executor

1. Familiarity with Decedent
2. Good Judgment
3. Organizational Skills
4. Communication Skills
5. Business Skills
6. Honesty and Integrity
7. Patience
8. Follow Up
9. Attention to Detail
10. Decision Making

Executor Bond

Unfortunately, all Executors cannot be trusted to do the right thing on behalf of the estate.

Also, some probate courts and Wills require a Bond to act as an insurance policy that will reimburse the estate in the event the Executor financially damages the estate and its beneficiaries.

CHAPTER 10

Don't be a Probate Statistic

Although death is inevitable, the unexpected nature of it has a broad reach. Therefore, it requires education, integrity, unity, and leadership of those involved to cushion the blow.

Plus, this is a very vulnerable time for the family and many of them are exploited by predators who take advantage of the grieved state, lack of planning and ignorance of widows, widowers, Executors, and other decision makers.

After my father passed, my mom was bombarded with predators who took advantage of her. She was fiercely independent but it was obvious that she was not skilled or emotionally prepared to deal with the finances and decisions that are required after the death of a loved one.

Fortunately, we were able to step in and help her protect her finances and secure the estate so she could enjoy a stress-free quality of life.

Also, please seek professional counsel from qualified representatives.

For example, there are Certified Elder Law Attorneys (CELA).

These are specialists that, according to our research, are required to pass an exam and verify their concentration in Elder Law.

CHAPTER 11

The Cost of Probate Miseducation, Fear, and Procrastination

There is a lot of miseducation, fear, procrastination, and indifference when it comes to estate planning.

As a result, many families are not prepared for the legal and financial responsibilities or the emotional burden of death.

The cost of probate can vary depending on the size and complexity of the estate.

Some of our clients pay less than $1000.00 to their estate attorney. However, many professionals charge by the hour, so the better prepared you are, the more money, time, and stress you save.

Also, some families order more funeral services than they can afford.

We have heard of instances where families take out mortgages for a two hour event to bury loved ones.

A funeral should be a planned expense and the Executor should receive a list of options and prices so he/she can make quality decisions. Also remember to check the invoice of services rendered after the funeral. There are many examples of extra fees, unauthorized charges, and overpayment of insurance that go unnoticed. You must inspect what you expect at every phase.

In addition to the high cost of funerals, many families are emotionally torn apart due to the disagreements that can arise when the wishes of the decedent are not clear.

This emotional stress can lead to disease, depression, discourse, disruption, and many preventable consequences.

CHAPTER 12

What is Probate?

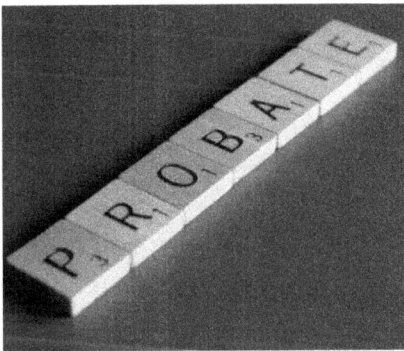

You've heard the phrase, "you can't take it with you?" That phrase is a probate reality because dead people cannot own assets. Therefore, the goal of probate is to secure legal permission to dispose of the assets and pay the bills of the decedent. According to Secure Law, PC, "probate is a court procedure by which a WILL is proved to be valid, after your death. It is only at this time that your WILL becomes a legal document in full force. Probate is also a term used today to describe the complete process of administration of your estate by the courts and your Personal Representative."

The goal of probate is for the Executor or the Court Appointed Administrator to receive court approval to legally act on behalf of the decedent.

Each state has different laws, "probate codes," as well as laws for "intestate succession" which occurs when a decedent dies without a Will. The Will must be validated by the court because it can be contested. Once the Will is validated, the Executor receives the Letters Testamentary to sign on behalf of the decedent for bank accounts, insurance information, real estate contracts, etc. If there is not a Will, an Administrator is assigned. This process can take days or years depending on the circumstances.

12 Pitfalls that Can Cost the Estate Thousands

Whether you are currently in probate or taking the powerful initiative to perform critical estate planning, this blueprint will be your trusted guide.

These are the Top 12 Pitfalls that can Cost the Estate Thousands:

1. The Estate is Not Probated
2. The Decedent Does Not Have a Will
3. The Will Cannot be Located
4. The Will is Ruled Invalid
5. The Will is Contested
6. The Beneficiaries Cannot be Located
7. The Executor is Dishonest and/or Unable to Serve
8. The Executor Does Not Receive Court Approval to Transfer Assets
9. Guardianship for Minors is Not Established
10. The Personal Property is Not Appraised
11. The Title to Personal Property Such as Vehicles is Nontransferable
12. The Real Estate May Not Be Able to Be Conveyed, Listed, and/or Sold

7 Steps to Probate Success

These are general steps that apply to most cases. Please consult an estate attorney for your specific situation.

1. Secure the Original Will and /or Codicils (Legal Updates to Will) and Death Certificate

The estate attorney will usually request the original copy of the Will and/or Codicils and Certificate of Death.

If there is not a Will, the court will assign an Administrator that will settle the estate based on the laws of intestate succession.

2. Secure an Attorney With Estate Experience

The attorney will provide you the documentation to file a petition to open probate.

This petition is usually filed with the probate court in the county where the decedent lived or owned property. The attorney will prepare the documentation for the probate court to review and counsel you on the process.

If the Will, Codicils, statements of heirs, and all required documentation is in order, you will receive your court approved authorization (Letters Testamentary or Letters of Administration) so you can sign as the legal representative for the estate.

This documentation is needed so the Personal Representative/Executor can execute real estate contracts, open accounts, close accounts, access information, etc.

This part can go quickly or it could take years if there are disputes regarding the validity of the Will, lack of cooperation between heirs, etc.

3. Evaluate Estate Assets

Many states require that the Executor submit a written report to the court listing everything the decedent owned along with each asset's value; as well as a notation as to how that value was obtained.

Real Estate can be appraised to determine real property value or a Broker Price Opinion (BPO) can be used.

When necessary, an independent appraiser is hired by the estate to appraise non-cash assets such as art, jewelry, antiques, furniture, etc.

4. Provide Notice to Creditors

The probate court's objective is to ensure the deceased's debts, taxes, and other valid claims are paid out of his or her estate before any distribution is made to the estate's beneficiaries.

The estate attorney will counsel the Executor on the best way to give legal, written notice to all creditors of the estate based upon state law. This gives any creditor who wishes to make a claim on the assets of the estate a limited time to do so. Credit reports from Equifax, Experian, and Transunion will help identify creditors. A consumer can obtain one free copy from each bureau at www.annualcreditreport.com

5. Pay Estate and Funeral Expenses, Debts, and Taxes

A creditor may also file a claim against the estate if they feel they are legally owed.

The Executor must determine which creditor's claims are legitimate and pay those along with other final bills from the estate.

In some instances, the Executor is permitted to open an account and sell estate assets to satisfy the decedent's obligations.

6. Distribute the Estate to Beneficiaries

Following the waiting period to allow creditors to file claims against the estate, and after all approved claims and bills are paid, generally, the personal representative petitions the court for the authority to transfer the remaining assets to beneficiaries as directed in the decedent's last will and testament.

7. Distribute the Real Estate before closing the estate.

Make sure the deed to transfer real estate to the beneficiaries is prepared and executed before closing the estate. This will ensure that the intended real estate beneficiaries receive proper title to the property.

Snapshot of the Probate Process

This is a snapshot of the probate process. You can see there is a lot more work to do if you do not have a court approved Will. More work equals more time and more money sucked from the estate. Plus, attorneys charge by the hour so the better prepared you are, the more money you save.

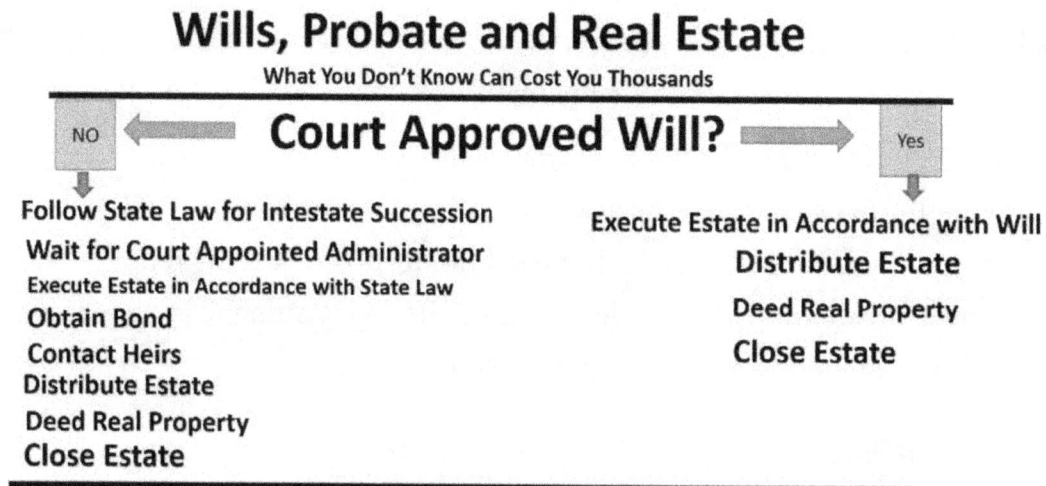

Wills, Probate and Real Estate
What You Don't Know Can Cost You Thousands

NO ← **Court Approved Will?** → Yes

Follow State Law for Intestate Succession

Wait for Court Appointed Administrator

Execute Estate in Accordance with State Law

Obtain Bond

Contact Heirs

Distribute Estate

Deed Real Property

Close Estate

Execute Estate in Accordance with Will

Distribute Estate

Deed Real Property

Close Estate

Sample Chart of Probate Process
Each state is different so contact an estate attorney for counseling
@2018 Sandra Brazelton and Alexandria Brazelton - All Rights Reserved

3 Money Saving Probate Real Estate Myth Busters

Myth 1 - I don't have an estate so I don't need a Will.

Myth Buster - Everyone needs a Will because everyone has an estate even though the value may vary.

Even if there is no real estate, life insurance, or cash available you need a Will. If you do not have a Will that provides valid instructions for the guardianship of minor children, the Court appointed administrator may make decisions that are not favorable to the family. Also, the Will provides critical instructions if there is simultaneous death.

Myth 2 - All Real Estate Agents have the same Real Estate Probate Experience

Myth Buster - Probate is a specialized area in which most real estate agents are not trained or experienced.

Most Executors would not go to a foot doctor for heart problems because they understand and value the expertise of a specialist.

Myth 3 – I am 65 so I no longer have to pay property taxes

Myth Buster – This exemption is based on age, income, disability status, and other factors. This information may qualify or disqualify you. Make sure you obtain this exemption, in writing, from the probate office before you stop paying your taxes.

We specialize in real estate probate and we can refer you to real estate agents in all locations to help you make sure they have the probate knowledge that you need.

7 Inside Secrets to Find Critical Probate Information

1. Find Insurance Policies and File Insurance Claims

Millions of dollars of estate wealth are lost because the insurance claim is not filed. Remember to check safe deposit boxes, home safes, online accounts, diaries, etc.

Also, some banks and organizations provide free policies that apply to accidental death and other areas so make sure you ask.

2. Obtain Credit Report to Find Creditors

As Executor, you must pay the creditors that you know of because you do not want an unpaid creditor to file a claim against the estate.

The three main reporting companies are Equifax, Experian, and Transunion.

You can obtain a free report at www.annualcreditreport.com to make sure you perform due diligence to contact creditors. This will help you avoid an unexpected creditor claim against the estate.

3. Check for Prepaid Burial Policies
4. Check Bank Statements for Auto Drafts, Deposits, and Payments to Creditors. Check the mail for bills and correspondence from creditors.
5. Check Pay Stubs for Income, Insurance Payments, IRA Contributions, Taxes, and Deductions
6. Obtain a Title Search on the Property to Make Sure any Liens are Valid and that No Other Liens Exist. This will save the estate a lot of time and money and will be invaluable when the property is listed.
7. Obtain a Title Search On the Decedent to Make Sure Any Liens Are Valid and That No Other Liens Exist. This will save the estate a lot of time and money and will be an invaluable when the property is listed.

CHAPTER 13

First Things First

The purpose of this 50-point checklist is to help the Personal Representative/Administrator manage all of the responsibilities associated with honoring the death of a loved one.

Once you review this information, make sure you gather all of the documentation and store a copy in the cloud for safe, fast, and easy access.

50 Point Checklist to Follow After Notification of Death

1	Obtain a legal pronouncement of death. In some areas this is done by the county coroner.
2	Provide a copy of Do Not Resuscitate Order if Emergency Personnel Are Called
3	Arrange for transportation to Morgue or Crematorium If no autopsy is needed, the body can be picked up by a mortuary (by law, a mortuary must provide price information over the phone)
4	Notify close family and friends (Ask someone to contact others – use decedents' cell phone for contacts)
5	Obtain original copies of death certificates (usually from the funeral home). Obtain multiple, original copies to provide to estate attorney, financial institutions, government agencies, and insurers, etc.
6	Notify doctor and other health care providers such as hospice, home health, etc.
7	Arrange for care of dependents
8	Notify Guardians of dependents

9	Contact Religious Organizations and ask about funeral/burial services
10	Collect Military Records and Contact Military Organizations, if Applicable, and ask about insurances and burial services support
11	Contact Sorority/Fraternity and Special Organizations and ask about insurances and burial services support
12	Secure Property
13	Change Locks
14	Protect All Assets
15	Secure the original copies of the Will and Codicils
16	Notify Pet Care Guardian
17	Arrange for care of pets including farm animals
18	Notify Veterinarian
19	Ask a friend or relative to keep an eye on the person's home, collect mail, throw food out, and water plants
20	Call the person's employer; Request info about benefits and any pay due from sick leave or vacation. Ask if there was a life-insurance policy through the company.
21	Arrange for funeral, family hour, burial, or cremation
22	Search the person's documents for an estate plan
23	Search the person's documents to find out whether there was a prepaid burial plan
24	Obtain an independent appraisal on jewelry, furs, art, collections, furniture, etc. if needed
25	Ask a friend or family member to go with you to the mortuary.
26	Meet with final care provider and obtain a detailed, written estimate of all funeral options and costs
27	Ask the final care provider for a written list and timeline of activities associated

	with the burial option you choose
28	Obtain independent estimates on the final care services you desire. The cost of caskets, vaults, crematory services, transportation, printing services, location, visitation, etc. are all areas of consideration and negotiation
29	Decide which services you want and negotiate the cost of Services
30	Prepare the obituary
31	Secure Hearing Aids, Glasses, Dentures, etc.
32	Contact a trust and estate attorney to open probate
33	Contact police and ask them to periodically check the decedent's house; especially if it is vacant
34	Contact Life insurance agent to terminate policy and to request claim forms
35	Contact Bank to find accounts and safe deposit boxes
36	Contact Agency providing pension services, to stop monthly check and get claim forms
37	Cancel Subscriptions – Cable, Internet, Cell Phone, Newspaper, Gym Memberships, etc.
38	Notify Child Care Facility
39	Cancel Health Insurance Payments
40	Cancel Long Term Care Arrangements
41	Contact postal service to stop or forward mail
42	Cancel Automatic Drafts
43	Contact the person's investment adviser, for information and claim forms on IRAs, Annuities, Stocks, Bonds, and other holdings
44	If necessary, the estate's Executor should open a bank account for the deceased's estate.
45	Pay All Bills – Mortgage, Utility, Car insurance, Loans, Credit cards, Car notes, student loans

46	Locate Keys to House, Vehicles, Office, etc.
47	Contact Social Security (800-772-1213; socialsecurity.gov) and other agencies from which the deceased received benefits, such as Veterans Affairs (800-827-1000; va.gov), to stop payments and ask about applicable survivor benefits
48	Close unused accounts
49	Pay Final Bills
50	Contact Accountant or tax preparer to find out whether an estate-tax return or final income-tax return should be filed. File State and Federal Taxes Check Federal Income Capital Gains Exemption

Probate and Contracting

Executing an estate requires the ability to contract on behalf of the decedent. Therefore, two of the qualifications we recommend for an Executor are basic business and organizational skills. These are 10 Probate Contracting Strategies to help ensure a successful probate experience:

10 Probate Contracting Strategies

1. Please read everything carefully before you sign anything
2. Obtain legal guidance to check all documentation
3. Obtain legal guidance for any questions
4. Obtain estimates on all services before you sign
5. Make sure you retain copies of everything you sign
6. Send all requests and notices by email with receipt verification
7. If notifications are mailed, make sure you use document tracking
8. Stay organized and inspect what you expect
9. Do not allow others to pressure you and do not make any decisions without emotional and legal clarity
10. Save and store information in the cloud for quick, safe, and convenient access

CHAPTER 14

Family, Emotions, and Probate

The probate process is stressful on everyone involved, especially the Executor.

Most Executors are not experienced in the probate process and they are serving under extremely stressful circumstances.

The emotions and expectations of family members may be turbulent and some of them can have selfish agendas to sabotage the estate and the wishes of the decedent.

We have experienced family members who commit fraud by changing the address on credit cards and other accounts so they could continue to use them. Some of them take property that was not meant for them; others forge the name of the decedent on legal documents and perform illegal acts that damage the estate and could result in criminal charges.

Also, many family members use this time to release stored anger from experiences that happened years ago. Much of this anger is directed at the Administrator because you are representing the decedent.

As Executor, it is your legal responsibility to protect the estate so some of your decisions may cause dissent. In your position, you may face anger, resentment, dishonesty, lack of cooperation, and other obstacles.

One solution is to educate the beneficiaries on all of your responsibilities so they can support you and not pressure you.

All of the beneficiaries benefit from a quick and correct probate process so keep them informed. Some families use conference calls, video chats, group messaging, Skype, etc. to keep everyone informed.

Do your best to lead with wisdom, forgiveness, courage, patience, honesty, open communication, and transparency. We also recommend spiritual and family counseling.

CHAPTER 15

Next Steps

The goal of Section 1 is to provide a comprehensive overview of the probate process and to empower you with some tools, strategies, and resources to manage the estate.

Section 2 will allow you to manage your own estate planning goals so you can make clear choices right now. It has over 40 worksheets for you to use to document your wishes and to gather critical information that your Executor and family will need.

It also contains information on preparing a Will, Durable Power of Attorney, and a Health Care Directive that was provided by Attorney Scott A. Rogers at Secure Law, PC in Huntsville, Alabama.

These documents will save you time, money, stress, and anxiety when you meet with your estate attorney.

Take Action Now!

Do not risk the security of your family.

You have shown powerful self-leadership by taking the time to review this blueprint.

However, you do not know when your family will have to take this journey on your behalf. Therefore, take the time right now to complete your Will and secure it in a safe place.

If you already have a Will, check to see if there are updates needed so you can create a Codicil. If major updates are needed, consider creating a new Will.

Please follow the 10 Step Probate Check-up Instructions.

Your executors and family will be forever grateful for your love, wisdom, guidance, and leadership.

CHAPTER 16

10 Step Probate Checkup Instructions

These are 10 preparation steps to save time, stress, and money before and during probate.

1. Meet with your Estate Attorney to Obtain a Legal Review of the Language and Intent of the Will and Codicils and Update them Accordingly
   a. This consultation can save a lot of time, money, and stress because the attorney may be able to clear up ambiguities and ensure the specific intent of the testator is properly documented. Plus, the established relationship will provide additional peace of mind.
2. Once the Will is updated, send it to the Attorney to ensure the Testator and Witness Signatures are Correct
3. Update the Will to Allow for Changes in Wishes, Law, Beneficiaries, etc.

This is critical after a divorce or death because beneficiaries of life insurance policies may not be able to be changed through a Will.

Also, there may be real and personal property that you want to keep under family control.

Keep the Will as current as possible so the Executor will be able to obtain Letters Testamentary without expensive and time consuming hearings.

4. Discuss Medicaid Strategies

Many families are disqualified from receiving Medicaid for their loved ones because they do not qualify. If Medicaid assistance is needed be sure you understand and comply with the requirements for income and real estate disposition. For example, according to elder law, real estate cannot be in the name of the recipient five years before the Medicaid service is requested. However, a good estate attorney can help you with different estate planning strategies such as a living trust so you can better prepare.

5. Update Insurance and Investment Beneficiaries

Many financial accounts such as 401 (k), IRAs, life insurance, retirement accounts, annuities, etc. pass at your death by contractual beneficiary.

    a. This means that whoever you name in your Will to receive these proceeds is irrelevant because the beneficiary designation has already been determined.

    b. There are plenty of stories where ex-spouses received life insurance and investment proceeds because the beneficiary was never changed.

A consistent review with your custodial manager will help you keep this current.

6. Provide Easy Access to Documents

Your Will and life insurance documents should not be stored in a safe deposit box unless someone you trust has shared access. This is because most banks seal safe-deposit boxes upon notification of death and it could take a long time to access the contents.

7. Consider a Long Term Care Insurance Policy

A long-term care policy will cover the expense and stress of caring for loved ones. The cost of long term care can range from thousands to tens of thousands monthly. Most family members are not financially able to cover these expenses and Medicaid has very strict qualifications. Even if the loved one is at home, the expense and responsibility can be overwhelming.

8. Research Extended Living Facilities in Advance

Sometimes the home may not be safe and accessible for either party.

In addition, your loved one should have a good quality of life.

Extended living facilities provide care, support, safety, and recreation to your loved one.

9. Conduct an Estate Sale

This can help you liquidate items that you do not plan to donate.

10. Make sure your Wills and Codicils are Enforceable in your State

There are a lot of online options that allow you to complete your Will and other estate planning documentation. However, if these are not compliant with your state law, your Will and other estate planning documents could be ruled invalid and unenforceable. If this happens, you may have to follow the same expensive and time consuming steps that intestate petitioners face.

When Should I Change My Will?

Please review this 9 step guide provided by Attorney Scott A. Rogers of Secure Law, PC in Huntsville, Alabama

When Should I Change my Will? When any of the following occur:

1) After a substantial change in the value of your assets;
2) Upon the birth or death of a member of your family;
3) Upon moving to a different legal residence state or a foreign country;
4) When the Personal Representative named in your Will dies or can no longer be considered competent;
5) When a guardian for a minor child must be named or when a new guardian must be appointed;
6) When your estate reaches a value level where it is no longer desirable to allow a child or beneficiary to exercise full control over the share, which he or she will receive after your death;
7) When you marry, re-marry, divorce, or separate;
8) When provisions of your Will no longer apply or need to be changed;
9) When you acquire additional property of higher value.

Compliments of Attorney Scott A. Rogers of Secure Law, PC in Huntsville, AL

CHAPTER 17

Section 2: Estate Planning Workbook

"A Good Man Leaves an Inheritance to His Children's Children: and the Wealth of the Sinner is Laid Up for the Just." Proverbs 13:22 KJV

Leaving an inheritance is a spiritual mandate. There are many types of inheritances such as work ethic and integrity but this inheritance specifically relates to wealth. This says a good man or woman leaves an inheritance. To us this implies that a bad man or woman does not leave an inheritance. In fact, we had a close family member who refused estate planning. Her attitude was "just let them fight over it". That is really a shackled and selfish mindset because death should be a celebration of your life. However, if you intentionally neglect your affairs, your legacy will be tainted and your influence will be weakened. When we experience this indifferent attitude, we pray for those individuals because "to him that knoweth to do good and doeth it not, to him it is sin." James 4:17

Please take the high road and trust the blessings of leaving an inheritance by fulfilling this mandate.

Section 2 of this blueprint is a comprehensive, estate planning work book to help you document critical information, protect the assets of the estate, and provide peace of mind to the family. It provides guidance, support, and instructions to help your love circle of family members, attorneys, physicians, etc. honor your wishes.

Therefore, the more thorough the content that you provide in this workbook, the more money you save and the less stress your loved ones' experience.

Many problems can be resolved when everyone is thinking clearly. Also, the estate will save a lot of time and money. Therefore, this information should be discussed and shared wisely.

If you are currently in probate, this workbook will help you identify the information you will need to settle the estate.

If you are not currently in probate, and even if you do not have a Will, the information and strategies will better prepare you to avoid many of the financial pitfalls associated with improper probate preparation and administration.

This section also provides information on preparing a Will, Durable Power of Attorney, and Health Care Directive and Health Care Proxy provided by Attorney Scott A. Rogers of Secure Law, PC in Huntsville, Alabama.

This information will help you when you meet with your estate attorney to finalize these critical documents.

We have also included over 40 worksheets to help you identify family members, assets, liabilities, and estate management strategies to complete your Estate Planning Workbook.

Estate Planning Workbook

Property of

_____

Date Created

_____

Date of Update 1   _____

Date of Update 2   _____

Date of Update 3   _____

Disclaimer

This blueprint provides reader with basic information on estate planning and financial management. This workbook does not provide legal advice. Please consult an estate attorney.

Estate Workbook Instructions and Warning

1. The contents of this workbook are very personal, confidential, and sensitive. The information you provide could damage you severely if it falls into the wrong hands. It can be used to steal identity, hack passwords, open accounts, access accounts, etc. Please make sure you protect your information and store this document in a safe place.
   Warning! The author is not responsible for the accuracy or security of any information you provide.
2. Scan a copy to a secure cloud based system for easy, safe, and secure access.
3. Make sure your Personal Representative, Executor, attorney, or other trusted source can access it
4. Review this blueprint annually and update it if there are changes to your wishes and/or beneficiaries.

Notes

Estate Plan Goals and Survey

Do you have an existing Will? Yes: _____ No: _____

Location

_____

_____

Do you have an existing Living Trust? Yes: _____ No: _____

Location

_____

_____

Do you have a prepaid burial plot? Yes _____ No _____

Location

_____

_____

Do you have burial insurance? Yes _____ No _____

Location

_____

_____

Do you have life insurance? Yes _____ No _____

Location

_____

_____

Do you have an existing Living Will/Health Directives?

Yes: _____ No: _____

Location

_____

Do you have an existing Power of Attorney? Yes: _____ No: _____

Location

_____

_____

Do you have an existing Healthcare POA/Proxy/Surrogate?

Yes: _____ No: _____

Location

_____

_____

Do you have a long term care policy? Yes: _____ No: _____

Location

_____

_____

Comments/Notes

_____

_____

Previous Will/Codicil Information

Date Created _____

Location

_____

_____

Codicil: Yes ____ No ____ Date Created _____

Location

_____

_____

Reason for Changing

_____

_____

Workbook Priorities and Concerns

I am concerned with the following issues:

- ☐ Providing income for a surviving spouse, partner, or beneficiary
- ☐ Paying for a child's education
- ☐ Providing for a special needs child
- ☐ Making a charitable bequest
- ☐ Estate planning for your business
- ☐ Disinheriting an heir
- ☐ Establishing a trust fund for a child or other individual
- ☐ Medicaid planning
- ☐ Estate taxes
- ☐ Gift taxes
- ☐ Arranging continuing care for pets/animals

Other Comments/Notes

_____

Notes

Personal Information Profile

No one else knows your information and wishes better than you.

Therefore, please take your time and complete this information as thoroughly as possible. Please record the information as accurately as possible and secure the documents that apply to each question.

This information will provide guidance in critical areas to help your family honor your wishes. It will also identify beneficiaries and protect your estate from predators and invalid claims against your estate.

Please consult an estate attorney if you have any questions and/or concerns.

Please include any additional information in the comments/notes section.

WARNING! Make sure you check the beneficiary on life-insurance policies, retirement accounts, etc. because these beneficiaries may not be able to be changed by WILLS.

Your Information

Your Full Legal Name_____

Age _____ Gender _____ Date of Birth _____

City, State, County of Birth

_____

Social Security Number

_____

Your Marital Status _____

(Single, Married, Divorced, Separated, Other) _____

Veteran? Yes _____ No _____ Military Service – Yes _____ No _____

Military Start Date _____ Military End Date _____

Type of Discharge _____

Email _____

Street Address_____

City _____

State _____ Zip: _____

Home/Cell Phone _____

Occupation _____

Monthly Salary $_____

Spouse Information

Spouse Full Legal Name _____

Date of Birth _____ Gender _____

City, State, County of Birth

_____

Social Security Number

_____

Veteran? Yes _____ No _____ Military Service – Yes _____ No _____

Military Start Date _____ Military End Date _____

Type of Discharge _____

Email _____

Street Address_____

City _____

State _____ Zip: _____

Home/Cell Phone _____

Occupation _____

Monthly Salary $_____

Business Information

Name of Business

_____

Business Address

_____

_____

_____

_____

Business Phone _____

Supervisor _____

Comments/Notes

_____

_____

_____

_____

_____

_____

Children Information

Total Number of All Children _____

Total Number of All Grand Children _____

Total Number of All Great Grand Children _____

Total Number of All Great, Great Grand Children _____

Total Number of All Step Children _____

Total Number of All Foster Children _____

Marriage Summary

Number of Marriages _____

Number of Children from All Marriages _____

Number of Divorces _____

Please provide information on Prenuptial or Postnuptial agreements

_____

_____

_____

Divorce Information

Please complete this information on/for all previous marriages

Date of Divorce _____

City, State, County of Divorce

_____

Ex-spouse Information

Full Name of Ex-Spouse

_____

Date of Birth _____ Gender _____

City, State, County of Birth

_____

Social Security Number

_____

Veteran? Yes _____ No _____ Military Service – Yes _____ No _____

Military Start Date _____ Military End Date _____

Type of Discharge _____

Email _____

Street Address_____

City _____

State _____ Zip: _____

Home/Cell Phone _____

Occupation _____

Monthly Salary $_____

Name of Business_____

Business Address

_____

Business Phone _____

Supervisor _____

Number of Years Married to Ex-Spouse _____

Total Number of Children with this Ex-Spouse _____

Total Number of Grand Children with this Ex-Spouse _____

Total Number of Great Grand Children with this Ex-Spouse _____

Total Number of Great, Great Grand Children with this Ex-Spouse _____

Total Number of Step Children with this Ex-Spouse _____

Total Number of Foster Children with this Ex-Spouse _____

WARNING! Make sure you check the beneficiary on life-insurance policies, retirement accounts, etc. because these beneficiaries may not be able to be changed by Will. Please consult an estate attorney for specific instructions.

Estimate of Estate Value

Assets		Liabilities	
Total Value of All Real Estate		Balance on All Mortgages	
Total Value of all Securities Stock, bonds, IRA		Balance on Vehicles	
Total value of life insurance		Balance on Credit Cards	
Cash value of life insurance		Balance of Student Loans	
Total value of business		Balance on Other Loans	
Total value of vehicles		Time Share	
Total value of jewelry, art, coins, collections, etc.		Child Support	
Total value of furniture		Doctors	
Total value of personal property		Insurances	
Total value of animals/livestock		Equipment	
Total value of intellectual property		All Creditors	
Other		Other	
Total		Total	
Total Both Columns	$		
Subtract Liabilities From Assets		Estimated Estate Value	$

Comments/Notes

_____

_____

Notes

List of Creditors

This is a Sample List of Creditors and an Outline of the Information that should be recorded on Each One

Mortgage Company	Furniture
Time Share	Utility
Student Loans	Cable
Vehicles	Phone
Loans	Insurances: Life, Health, Disability
Credit Cards	Car Insurance
Business Loans	Child Care
Equipment	Other
Other	
Required Information: Name of Company Account Number Balance Due Date Due Address of Company Phone Number Point of Contact Email **Purpose of Account**	Utility Bill Name of Company Property Address of Bill Account Number Balance Due Date Due Address of Company Phone Number Point of Contact **Email**

Notes

☐ _____

☐ _____

☐ _____

☐ _____

☐ _____

☐ _____

☐ _____

☐ _____

☐ _____

☐ _____

☐ _____

☐ _____

☐ _____

☐ _____

☐ _____

☐ _____

☐ _____

☐ _____

☐ _____

☐ _____

Real Estate Information

Please Complete this Information for Each Piece of Real Estate

Name of Deeded Owner (S)	
Address of Property	
Type of Property	
Legal Description	
How is Title Held	
Date Purchased	
Purchase Price	
Date Sold	
Sales Price	
Closing Attorney	
Current Balance	
Mortgage Company	
Account Number	
Type of Mortgage	
Mortgage Company Address	
Mortgage Company Phone	
Mortgage Company Email	
Number of Years Of Mortgage	
Current Use of Property	
Location of Settlement Statement	

Comments/Notes _____

Notes

☐ _____

☐ _____

☐ _____

☐ _____

☐ _____

☐ _____

☐ _____

☐ _____

☐ _____

☐ _____

☐ _____

☐ _____

☐ _____

☐ _____

☐ _____

☐ _____

☐ _____

☐ _____

☐ _____

☐ _____

☐ _____

Business Ownership Information

Name	
Address	
Type of Business	
Business Start Date	Insurance
Business Termination Date	Workman's Comp
Business Value	Vehicles
Business Assets	Accounting
Business Liabilities	Taxes
Rents	Lines of Credit
Leases	Accounts Payable
Contracts	Accounts Receivable
Other	

Comments/Notes

Notes

☐ _____

☐ _____

☐ _____

☐ _____

☐ _____

☐ _____

☐ _____

☐ _____

☐ _____

☐ _____

☐ _____

☐ _____

☐ _____

☐ _____

☐ _____

☐ _____

☐ _____

☐ _____

☐ _____

Safe Deposit Box Information

WARNING! – Original forms of Wills, life insurance policies, and other documents should not be stored in a safe deposit box unless someone else you trust is authorized to access the account and knows where the keys are located. This is because most banks seal safe-deposit boxes upon notification of death and it could take a long time to access the contents.

A fire proof home safe is a good alternative. However, make sure someone you trust can access it.

Bank Name/Branch	
Bank Address	
Box Owner	
Box Number	
Box Key Location	
Individuals With Access	

Comments/Notes_____

Home Safe Information

Location	
Combination	
Contents	
Location of Other Information	
Description of Other Information: Off Shore Account, Private Account, etc.	

73

Notes

☐ _____

☐ _____

☐ _____

☐ _____

☐ _____

☐ _____

☐ _____

☐ _____

☐ _____

☐ _____

☐ _____

☐ _____

☐ _____

☐ _____

☐ _____

☐ _____

☐ _____

☐ _____

☐ _____

☐ _____

☐ _____

Household/Personal Valuables Inventory List

This Inventory List Will Help You Value Your Estate. Please update it as Items are Bought, Sold, or Discarded

ITEM	LOCATION	DATE OF PURCHASE	MODEL/ SERIAL NUMBER	COST	CURRENT VALUE

Notes

Insurance Policy Information

Please Complete This Information for All Insurance Policies

WARNING! – Original forms of Wills, life insurance policies, and other documents should not be stored in a safe deposit box unless someone else you trust is authorized to access the account and knows where the keys are located.

This is because most banks seal safe-deposit boxes upon notification of death and it could take a long time to access the contents.

A fire proof home safe is a good alternative. However, make sure someone you trust can access it.

Remember to list all insurance policies including accidental death, cancer, and mortgage pay off policies.

Name of Insurance Company	
Address of Insurance Company	
Insurance Company Phone	
Insurance Agent Name	
Insurance Company Email	
Type of Policy	
Policy Number	
Policy Value	
Policy Status	
Date Policy Issued	
Date Policy Ended	
Cost of Policy	
Cash Value of Policy	
Beneficiary	

Comments _____

Notes

☐ _____

☐ _____

☐ _____

☐ _____

☐ _____

☐ _____

☐ _____

☐ _____

☐ _____

☐ _____

☐ _____

☐ _____

☐ _____

☐ _____

☐ _____

☐ _____

☐ _____

☐ _____

☐ _____

☐ _____

Retirement Accounts

Please Complete this Information for all Retirement Accounts, Ira's, etc.

Name on Retirement Account	
Name of Account Custodian	
Address of Account Custodian	
Phone Number of Custodian	
Email of Account Custodian	
Type of Account	
Account Number	
Original Deposit Amount	
Date Opened	
Date Closed	
Beneficiary of Account	
Name of Account Representative	

Comments/Notes

_____

_____

_____

_____

_____

_____

Please Complete this Information for all Retirement Accounts, IRA's, etc.

Name on Retirement Account	
Name of Account Custodian	
Address of Account Custodian	
Phone Number of Custodian	
Email of Account Custodian	
Type of Account	
Account Number	
Original Deposit Amount	
Date Opened	
Date Closed	
Account Beneficiary	
Name of Account Representative	

Comments/Notes

_____

_____

_____

_____

_____

Online and Electronic Account Information

Many creditors and accounts are managed online so this information is critical to settling the estate without overlooking creditors and missing valuable assets.

This information can save the family and the probate process a lot of time, stress, and money.

Name of Account	User Name	Password	Security Questions	Security Answers

Electronic Device Access	User Name	Password	Security Questions	Security Answers
IPAD				
Home Computer				
Work Computer				
Phone				
Email				
Other				

Notes

☐ _____

☐ _____

☐ _____

☐ _____

☐ _____

☐ _____

☐ _____

☐ _____

☐ _____

☐ _____

☐ _____

☐ _____

☐ _____

☐ _____

☐ _____

☐ _____

☐ _____

☐ _____

☐ _____

Personal Property Estate Distribution Instructions

This is the list of names and instructions of Individuals or Organizations that you designate as beneficiaries of personal property of your estate.

83

Notes

- _____
- _____
- _____
- _____
- _____
- _____
- _____
- _____
- _____
- _____
- _____
- _____
- _____
- _____
- _____
- _____
- _____
- _____
- _____
- _____
- _____

Real Property Distribution Instructions

This is the list of names and instructions of Individuals or Organizations that you designate as beneficiaries of real property of your estate.

Full Legal Name of Real Property Beneficiary

Relationship

_____

Address

_____

City_____ State _____

County _____ Zip _____

Phone _____

Social Security Number

_____

Gender _____ Date of Birth _____

Date of Death _____

Email

_____

Property Legal Description, Address, Plat, Survey, etc.

_____

_____

_____

Full Legal Name of Real Property Beneficiary

Relationship

_____

Address

_____

City_____ State _____

County _____ Zip _____Phone _____

Social Security Number

_____

Gender_____ Date of Birth _____

Date of Death _____

Email

_____

Property Legal Description, Address, Plat, Survey, etc.

_____

_____

_____

Disinheritance Information

This is the list of names that you willfully exclude and cut out as beneficiaries of any assets from your estate.

Full Legal Name of Disinherited Heir

_____

Relationship

_____

Address

_____

City_____ State _____

County _____ Zip _____Phone _____

Social Security Number

_____

Gender_____ Date of Birth _____

Date of Death _____

Email

_____

Notes

Location of Important Documents

This is a summary of the documentation for you to complete and share with your Executor, attorney, and love circle so you will have the information to draft your Will and make your wishes known.

Remember to save copies of all original documentation to a Google drive or cloud for immediate access.

WARNING! – Original forms of Wills, life insurance policies, and other documents should not be stored in a safe deposit box unless someone else you trust is authorized to access the account and knows where the keys are.

This is because most banks seal safe-deposit boxes upon notification of death and it could take a long time to access the contents.

A fire proof home safe is a good alternative. However, make sure someone you trust can access it.

Document	Location of Original Copy
Adoption Papers	
Vehicles	
Bank Statements	
Real Estate Documents	
Religious Documents	
Birth Certificates	
Business Contracts	
Child Guardianship	
Canceled Checks	
Credit Card Statements	

Death Certificates	
Property Deeds	
Divorce Papers	
Driver's License Info	
Educational Transcripts	
Employee Benefit Documents	
Family Tree	
Funeral And Burial Plans	
Household Inventory	
Income Records	
Income Tax Returns	
Insurance Policies	
Legal and Accounting	
Marriage Certificates	
Medical Information	
Military Documents (DD-214)	
Important Contacts	
Mortgage Papers	
Online and Electronic Account Information	

Passports	
Pension Plan Records	
People to Notify	
Personal and Family Data Profile	
Estate Distribution Instructions	
Real Estate Distribution Instructions	
Personal Property Distribution Instructions	
Religious Restrictions	
Prepaid Burial Policy	
Receipts	
Securities	
Social Security Cards	
Stock/Bond Certificates	
Warranties	
Will/Estate Plans/Codicils	
Other	
Other	
Other	
Other	

Comments/Notes

Notes

Medical Information

Please Complete this Information for Doctors, Dentists, Specialists, etc.
YOUR NAME _____
Blood Type _____ Organ Donor: Yes_____ No _____
NAME of DOCTOR/DENTIST/SPECIALIST _____ DOCTOR PHONE _____
PHYSICIAN ADDRESS
PHYSICIAN EMAIL
PRESCRIBED MEDICINES
ALLERGIES/SPECIAL CONDITIONS/INSTRUCTIONS
NAME of DOCTOR/DENTIST/SPECIALIST _____ DOCTOR PHONE _____
PHYSICIAN ADDRESS
PHYSICIAN EMAIL
PRESCRIBED MEDICINES
ALLERGIES/SPECIAL CONDITIONS/INSTRUCTIONS

Comments/Notes

Notes

☐ _____

☐ _____

☐ _____

☐ _____

☐ _____

☐ _____

☐ _____

☐ _____

☐ _____

☐ _____

☐ _____

☐ _____

☐ _____

☐ _____

☐ _____

☐ _____

☐ _____

☐ _____

☐ _____

☐ _____

Family Tree

This section is for information on parents, grandparents, siblings, and children.

This information should be as thorough as possible to ensure all heirs are accounted for and to protect the estate from unlawful claims. It will also help in notifying those in your love circle and in preparing your obituary. You can use social media, family reunion booklets, online ancestry services, wedding information, birth certificates, death certificates, bible records, testimonials, online ancestry search companies, etc. to find and record information.

YOUR PARENTS
FATHER'S FULL LEGAL NAME
_____
Address
_____
City_____ State _____
County_____ Zip _____Phone _____
Social Security Number _____
Date of Birth _____ Date of Death _____
Email
_____

PATERNAL FATHER'S FULL LEGAL NAME

_____

Address

_____

City_____ State _____

County_____ Zip _____Phone _____

Social Security Number

_____

Date of Birth _____ Date of Death _____

Email

_____

PATERNAL MOTHER'S FULL LEGAL NAME

_____

Address

_____

City_____ State _____

County _____ Zip _____Phone _____

Social Security Number

_____

Date of Birth _____ Date of Death _____

Email

_____

FATHER'S SIBLING FULL LEGAL NAME

_____

Address

_____

City_____ State _____

County _____ Zip _____Phone _____

Social Security Number _____

Gender _____ Date of Birth _____

Date of Death _____

Email

_____

—

FATHER'S SIBLING FULL LEGAL NAME

_____

Address

_____

City_____ State _____

County _____ Zip _____Phone _____

Social Security Number _____

Gender _____ Date of Birth _____

Date of Death _____

Email

_____

Notes

☐ _____

☐ _____

☐ _____

☐ _____

☐ _____

☐ _____

☐ _____

☐ _____

☐ _____

☐ _____

☐ _____

☐ _____

☐ _____

☐ _____

☐ _____

☐ _____

☐ _____

☐ _____

☐ _____

MOTHER'S FULL LEGAL NAME

_____

Address

_____

City_____ State _____

County _____ Zip _____Phone _____

Social Security Number _____

Gender _____ Date of Birth _____

Date of Death _____

Email

_____

MATERNAL FATHER'S FULL LEGAL NAME

_____

Address

_____

City_____ State _____

County _____ Zip _____Phone _____

Social Security Number _____

Gender _____ Date of Birth _____

Date of Death _____

Email

_____

MATERNAL MOTHER'S FULL LEGAL NAME

_____

Address

_____

City_____ State _____

County _____ Zip _____Phone _____

Social Security Number

_____

Date of Birth _____ Date of Death _____

Email

_____

MOTHER'S SIBLING FULL LEGAL NAME

_____

Address

_____

City_____ State _____

County _____ Zip _____Phone _____

Social Security Number _____

Gender _____ Date of Birth _____

Date of Death _____

Email

_____

MOTHER'S SIBLING FULL LEGAL NAME

_____

Address

_____

City_____ State _____

County _____ Zip _____Phone _____

Social Security Number _____

Gender _____ Date of Birth _____

Date of Death _____

Email

_____

Notes

☐ _____

☐ _____

☐ _____

☐ _____

☐ _____

☐ _____

☐ _____

☐ _____

☐ _____

☐ _____

☐ _____

☐ _____

☐ _____

☐ _____

☐ _____

☐ _____

☐ _____

☐ _____

☐ _____

☐ _____

YOUR CHILDREN

Full Legal Name of Child

_____

Address

_____

City_____ State _____

County _____ Zip _____Phone _____

Social Security Number _____

Gender _____ Date of Birth _____

Date of Death _____

Email

_____

Full Legal Name of Child

_____

Address

_____

City_____ State _____

County _____ Zip _____Phone _____

Social Security Number _____

Gender _____ Date of Birth _____

Date of Death _____

Email

_____

Full Legal Name of Child

_____

Address

_____

City_____ State _____

County _____ Zip _____Phone _____

Social Security Number _____

Gender_____ Date of Birth _____

Date of Death _____

Email

_____

Full Legal Name of Child

_____

–

Address

_____

City_____ State _____

County _____ Zip _____Phone _____

Social Security Number _____

Gender _____ Date of Birth _____

Date of Death _____

Email

_____

YOUR GRAND CHILDREN

Full Legal Name of Grand Child

_____

Address

_____

City_____ State _____

County _____ Zip _____Phone _____

Social Security Number _____

Gender _____ Date of Birth _____

Date of Death _____

Email

_____

Full Legal Name of Grandchild

_____

Address

_____

City_____ State _____

County _____ Zip _____Phone _____

Social Security Number _____

Gender _____ Date of Birth _____

Date of Death _____

Email

_____

YOUR GREAT, GREAT GRANDCHILDREN

Full Legal Name of Great, Great Grandchild

_____

Address

_____

City_____ State _____
County _____ Zip _____Phone _____
Social Security Number

_____

Gender _____ Date of Birth
_____

Date of Death _____
Email

_____

Full Legal Name of Great, Great Grand Child

_____

–

Address

_____

–

City_____ State _____
County _____ Zip _____Phone _____
Social Security Number

_____

Gender _____ Date of Birth _____
Date of Death _____
Email

_____

Executor Information

Executor of Will	
Name of Firm If Applicable	
Description of Executive Power	
Executor Address	
Executor Phone Number	
Executor Email	
Documents Held at Firm	

Comments/Notes

_____

_____

_____

_____

Alternate Executor Information

Alternate Executor of Will	
Name of Firm If Applicable	
Description of Executive Power	
Executor Address	
Executor Phone Number	
Executor Email	
Documents Held at Firm	

Notes

- [ ] _____
- [ ] _____
- [ ] _____
- [ ] _____
- [ ] _____
- [ ] _____
- [ ] _____
- [ ] _____
- [ ] _____
- [ ] _____
- [ ] _____
- [ ] _____
- [ ] _____
- [ ] _____
- [ ] _____
- [ ] _____
- [ ] _____
- [ ] _____
- [ ] _____
- [ ] _____

Guardian Information

Please Provide this Information for Each Child/Dependent.

This Area is Critical. Please Thoroughly Discuss all Aspects of Guardianship Including Religion, Education, Finances, Medical History, Goals, etc. Please Include all Information if Joint Guardianship Applies.

Child/Dependent Name	
Gender	
Date of Birth	
Social Security Number	
Doctor of Child/Dependent	
School of Child/Dependent	
Medical Information	
Activities	
Financial Resources	
Next of Kin of Child/Dependent	
Designated Guardian	
Guardian Address	
Guardian Phone	
Guardian Email	
Alternate Guardian	
Alternate Guardian Address	
Alternate Guardian Phone	
Alternate Guardian Email	
Key Information on Child/Dependent	

Notes

☐ _____

☐ _____

☐ _____

☐ _____

☐ _____

☐ _____

☐ _____

☐ _____

☐ _____

☐ _____

☐ _____

☐ _____

☐ _____

☐ _____

☐ _____

☐ _____

☐ _____

☐ _____

☐ _____

Banking Information

Please Complete this Information for all Accounts.

Name on Bank Account	
Name of Bank	
Address of Bank	
Phone Number	
Type of Account	
Email of Bank	
Account Number	
Date Opened	
Beneficiary of Account	
Name of Banker	

Banking Information

Name on Bank Account	
Name of Bank	
Address of Bank	
Phone Number	
Type of Account	
Email of Bank	
Account Number	

Beneficiary of Account	
Date Opened	
Name of Banker	

Legal Information

Please Complete this Information for all Legal Services

Attorney Name	
Firm Name	
Description of Services Provided	
Firm Address	
Firm Phone Number	
Firm Email	
Documents Held at Firm	

Attorney Name	
Firm Name	
Description of Services Provided	
Firm Address	
Firm Phone Number	
Firm Email	
Documents Held at Firm	

Notes

Accounting Information

Please Complete this Information for all Accounts.

Accountant Name	
Firm Name	
Description of Services Provided	
Firm Address	
Firm Phone Number	
Firm Email	

Comments/Notes

_____

_____

Accountant Name	
Firm Name	
Description of Services Provided	
Firm Address	
Firm Phone Number	
Firm Email	

Comments/Notes

_____

Notes

☐ _____

☐ _____

☐ _____

☐ _____

☐ _____

☐ _____

☐ _____

☐ _____

☐ _____

☐ _____

☐ _____

☐ _____

☐ _____

☐ _____

☐ _____

☐ _____

☐ _____

☐ _____

☐ _____

☐ _____

Power of Attorney Information

Name	
Address	
Phone	
Email	

Driver's License Information

Name on License	
License Number	
Social Security #	
Issue Date	
Expiration Date	
State of Issue	
Restrictions	
Other	

Comments/Notes_____

Passport Information

Name on Passport	
Passport Number	
Social Security #	
Issue Date	
Expiration Date	
State of Issue	
Restrictions	
Other	

Comments/Notes _____

Notes

Record of Education/Trade School and Training

Please Complete this Information for all Areas of Study, Trade, and Educational Accomplishments

High School Name/Address	
Name as Registered	
Dates Attended	
Field of Study	
Degree Obtained Yes/No _____	Type of Degree

Comments/Notes

_____

Record of Education/Trade School and Training

Name as Registered		
School Name/Address		
Dates Attended		
Field of Study		
Degree Obtained Yes/No _____	Type of Degree	

Comments/Notes _____

Record of Higher Education

Name as Registered		
School Name/Address		
Dates Attended		
Field of Study		
Degree Obtained Yes/No _____	Type of Degree	

Notes

Record of Employment

Please Complete this Information for all Areas of Employment

Name	
Employer Name/Address	
Title	
Employment Date	
Job Description	
Date Started	Date Ended
Starting Salary	Ending Salary

Comments/Notes

Record of Employment

Name	
Employer Name/Address	
Title	
Employment Date	
Job Description	
Date Started	Date Ended
Starting Salary	Ending Salary

Notes

- [ ] _____
- [ ] _____
- [ ] _____
- [ ] _____
- [ ] _____
- [ ] _____
- [ ] _____
- [ ] _____
- [ ] _____
- [ ] _____
- [ ] _____
- [ ] _____
- [ ] _____
- [ ] _____
- [ ] _____
- [ ] _____
- [ ] _____
- [ ] _____
- [ ] _____
- [ ] _____

Important Contacts

This is Your Quick Contact List of Important Contacts

Accountant		
Phone	Email	Address
Banker		
Phone	Email	Address
Financial Advisor		
Phone	Email	Address
Clergy		
Phone	Email	Address
Doctor		
Phone	Email	Address
Doctor		
Phone	Email	Address
Attorney		
Phone	Email	Address

Important Contacts Continued

Executor of Will		
Phone	Email	Address
Alternate Executor of Will		
Phone	Email	Address
Funeral Home Choice		
Phone	Email	Address
Insurance Agent		
Phone	Email	Address
Insurance Agent		
Phone	Email	Address
Fraternity/Sorority		
Phone	Email	Address
Other		
Phone	Email	Address

Comments/Notes

Pet Care Guardian Information

Name	
Address	
Phone	
Email	
Name of Pet	
Type of Pet	
Birthday of Pet	
Medical History	
Special Instructions	
Veterinarian Name	
Veterinarian Address	
Veterinarian Phone	
Veterinarian Email	

P.O. Box Information

Box Owner		
Address		
Box Number		
Box Key Location		
Individuals with Access		

Notes

Vehicle Information

Please Complete this Information for Each Vehicle, Boat, Airplane, Mobile Home, etc.

Name on Vehicle Title	
Make/Model	
Year	
Color	
Date Purchased	
Purchase Dealership/Person	
Purchase Price	
Date Sold	
Sold Price	
Person Sold to	

Vehicle Identification Number (VIN)

Comments/Notes

_____

_____

_____

_____

Vehicle Information

Please Complete this Information for Each Vehicle, Boat, Airplane, Mobile Home, etc.

Name on Vehicle Title	
Make/Model	
Year	
Color	
Date Purchased	
Purchase Dealership/Person	
Purchase Price	
Date Sold	
Sold Price	
Person Sold to	

Vehicle Identification Number (VIN)

Comments/Notes

_____

_____

_____

_____

_____

People to Notify

Please use this for quick access to family, friends, clergy, neighbors, vets, etc.

List the Names Here and Fill in the Individual Contact Information in the Next Section

Comments/Notes

Notes

Contact Information for People to Notify

Name of Person to Notify	
Address	
Phone	
Relationship	
Email	

Name of Person to Notify	
Address	
Phone	
Relationship	
Email	

Name of Person to Notify	
Address	
Phone	
Relationship	
Email	

Comments/Notes

_____

_____

Notes

- [ ]
- [ ]
- [ ]
- [ ]
- [ ]
- [ ]
- [ ]
- [ ]
- [ ]
- [ ]
- [ ]
- [ ]
- [ ]
- [ ]
- [ ]
- [ ]
- [ ]
- [ ]
- [ ]
- [ ]

Funeral and Burial Instructions

Location of Service	
Location of Burial	
Funeral Home Choice	
Singers/Songs	
Speakers	
Clothing Preference and Location of Clothing, Jewelry, etc.	
Viewing Choice Family Only, Public, None	
Burial/Cremation Choice	
Wishes for Remains of Ashes	
Location of Special Photos	
Special Requests	
Location of Burial Policy	

Comments/Notes

_____

_____

_____

Notes

Sample Will Instructions and Preparation Blueprint

Based on our research, we have identified sixteen areas for you to consider when you meet with your estate attorney to prepare or update your Will.

You should also receive counsel on how and when to discuss this with your family, Executor, alternates, beneficiaries, guardian of minor children, estate attorney, clergy, and others in your love circle.

Most of the information that you need to provide should be documented in Section 2 of the "Wills, Probate, and Real Estate" workbook.

Some of these provisions may not be applicable or lawful in your state. Therefore, it is critical that you seek legal guidance from an estate attorney because each state has different laws and an invalid Will can bankrupt your estate.

1	Title and Declaration
2	Marital History/Family History
3	Appointment of Executor and Alternate Executor and Instructions for Payment of Debts, Taxes, and Funeral Expenses out of the estate
4.	Funeral Arrangements/Instructions
5.	Guardian for Minor Children
6.	Trust for Minor Children
7.	Disinheritance Instructions
8.	Personal Property Bequeath Instructions
9.	Real Property Bequeath Instructions
10.	Residuary Clause
11.	Simultaneous Death of a Beneficiary
12.	No Contest Provision
13.	Severability Clause
14.	Signatures of Testator and Witnesses
15.	Additional Video Verification
16.	Notary Requirements

1. Title and Declaration

Typically stated "Last Will and Testament of Testator"
Declaration

    a. Full Name of Testator

    b. Complete Residential Address of Testator Including County of Residence

    c. Declaration of Legal Age

    d. Declaration of Capacity to Contract Will

    e. Declaration that the Document is the Last Will and Testament

    f. Declaration that Testator is Revoking all previous Wills and Codicils

    g. Declaration that Testator is not under Duress or undue Influence

    h. Codicils – Provide Name and Date of Codicils

2. Marital History/Family History

This section should state whether testator is married, divorced, widowed, separated, or in a common law marriage. It should also provide specific information on the current spouse and children if applicable.

3. Appointment of Executor and Alternate Executor and Instructions for Payment of Debts, Taxes, and Funeral Expenses

This provision should list the person or persons you want to file probate, manage your assets, and make sure the right people receive them. These are the people who generally have the best knowledge in terms of how the testator wants the estate distributed.

Typically, a person names the remaining spouse or main beneficiary of the estate as Executor. However, please check out the 10 recommended qualifications for an Executor because this is the most important position in an estate.

You should always list the powers you want your Executor and Trustee to have. If you do not list these powers, the simplest of tasks, such as selling your house may cost the estate a lot of money and take years to execute.

This provision should state exactly how debts, funeral expenses, and taxes are to be paid as well as which assets are used to pay them.

This provision should also include an Alternate Executor who will be in charge of the estate just in case the primary executor is unable or unwilling to serve.

4. Funeral Arrangements/Instructions

Funeral arrangements are usually included so testator can document their wishes. This can include specifics of the funeral location, funeral service, burial place, burial type, how the remains will be disposed, etc.

5. Guardian for Dependents

Guardianship of minor children is based on the age and other factors of the minor that vary by state.

The selection of guardianship is a major responsibility that should be planned and communicated in advance.

This section should include the name(s) of the person(s) who will be appointed legal guardian of the testator's children, should both the testator and spouse pass.

If the testator names a couple as legal guardians of the minor children, be sure to include both of their names. Also, make sure an Alternate Guardian is chosen.

6. Trust for Minor Children

A trust can be set up for a specific purpose such as the health, education, maintenance, and support of minor children. The testator can appoint a trustee as an individual, financial institution, business entity, etc. The testator can also instruct the age and distribution of trust funds. There are also advanced estate planning strategies that avoid probate for assets in trust. Please choose a Primary and Alternate Trustee when you consult an estate attorney.

7. Disinheritance Clause

A disinheritance clause is a provision in a Will disinheriting or cutting off an heir from any of the proceeds of the estate. The Will must clearly name the person being disinherited. This clause could cause the Will to be contested so please consult an estate attorney.

8. Personal Property Bequeath Instructions

This is probably the most important part of the Will.

Each beneficiary should be specifically named so there is no doubt as to the identity of the beneficiary. Please remember to use the full, legal name and any other details that would eliminate any confusion or misunderstanding.

This section should include specific instructions on how the testator wishes for the estate to be distributed among the specific organizations and people named as beneficiaries.

Remember, some assets such as joint survivorship title in real estate, payable-on-death life insurance policies, bank accounts, and trusts, etc. may already be assigned to beneficiaries.

Remember the Will becomes public record which means that anyone can read it.

Please make sure the Will is reviewed and updated consistently so that the assets can go to the intended beneficiary. It is also a good idea to name Alternate Beneficiaries in the event of the death of a beneficiary.

9. Real Property Bequeath Instructions

Real Property includes homes, farms, land, buildings, crops, etc. It is important to specifically describe the real property that is being bequeathed by legal description, address, survey, appraisal, and other identifying documentation.

10. Residuary Clause

This provision provides instructions for the distribution of any remaining estate assets.

11. Simultaneous Death of a Beneficiary

This is an important provision in case of unnatural death. It will allow the testator to dictate who died first so the estate can be distributed in accordance with testator wishes.

12. No Contest Provision

A no-contest clause is a clause which may be included in a Last Will and Testament or a Trust Agreement and generally provides that if a beneficiary contests any provision of the Will or Trust, that beneficiary will forfeit any interest he or she has in the estate or trust property.

13. Severability Clause

A severability clause refers to a contractual provision that describes the effect that an unenforceable part of a contract will have on an agreement.

14. Signatures and Verification of Testator and Witnesses

Improper signatures can void the validity of a Will and throw the entire process into an expensive and time consuming nightmare.

These are recommended best practices:

The testator should initial each page of the Will and sign the Will in front of qualified witnesses and in the presence of a qualified Notary.

The testator should print his/her name, provide the complete address, fill in the date of signing, and provide an email address. The witness language should also be correct in accordance with state law so please consult an estate attorney.

15. Video Verification

A video is a good way to capture the intent of the testator. Sometimes these are played at the reading of the Will so family members are reassured of the testator's wishes. It may also help answer questions and resolve conflict. The video can show the testator reading the information, initialing each page, and signing in front of the witnesses and notary. The video should be saved to a cloud based storage drive and copies provided to family, executor, attorney, etc.

16. Notary Requirements

In many states, the Will does not have to be notarized.

However, many probate courts accept "self-proving affidavits." This is a notarized document verifying that the testator and the witnesses signed the affidavit at the same time the Will is signed and witnessed.

A notarized, self-proving affidavit attached to your Will can potentially help it move more quickly through probate. However, they may not be valid in all states so check with an experienced estate attorney.

Notes

Estate Planning Information Packet

This estate planning information packet is from the law office of Attorney Scott A. Rogers of Secure Law in Huntsville, Alabama. It provides a template for you to complete your Will, Durable Power of Attorney, and Health Care Directive.

Please contact the law office of Attorney Scott A. Rogers listed below if you have any questions

Scott A. Rogers, Esq.

Secure Law PC

https://securelawpc.com

2310-A Market Place, Suite A

Huntsville, AL 35801

Phone (256) 513-8282 - FAX (256) 513-8203

Preparation of your WILL is a time consuming process; therefore, we must limit the number of drafts prepared on your behalf to three (3). We will prepare the document(s) according to your wishes. An additional charge will apply to each draft prepared after the third one is provided.

PLEASE USE CAREFUL CONSIDERATION WHEN MAKING YOUR DECISIONS!

Your Full Name

_____

Date of Birth _____

Social Security Number

_____

Complete Address

_____

_____

Email:

_____

Telephone: Home/Cell _____ _____

Work _____

Spouse's Full Name (if applicable)

_____

Date of Birth _____

Social Security Number

_____

Complete Address

_____

_____

Telephone: Home/Cell _____

Work _____

Email

_____

For Each Child, List His/Her:

Full Name

_____

Date of Birth _____ Gender _____

Marital Status _____

Address

_____

_____

Email _____

Cell/Work Phone

_____

Full Name

_____

Date of Birth _____ Gender _____

Marital Status

_____

Address

_____

_____

Email _____

Cell/Work Phone _____

Primary Guardian:

The guardian of your minor children will be the person whom you wish to have the actual custody of the children and be responsible for their care and upbringing. Please name a Primary Guardian and an Alternate Guardian and list their relationship to you.

Name

_____

Relationship to You _____

Complete Address

_____

_____

Email

_____

Cell/Work Phone

_____

Alternate Guardian:

Name

_____

Relationship to You _____

Complete Address

_____

_____

Email

_____

Cell/Work Phone

_____

Trustee Information:

The Trustee of your children will be the person whom you wish to control any financial assets and affairs and hold any property in their care until such age as you designate the children to receive their trust. This can be one person, two people, or a bank. Please name a Primary Trustee and an Alternate Trustee, their relationship to you, and the age at which your children will receive their trust. The Guardian and Trustee do not have to be the same.

If you wish your child(ren) to receive their trust in installments, please indicate age and percentage (e.g.: 50% at age 23, remainder at age 25).

Name of Child _____

Ages: _____, _____, _____

Percentages: _____, _____, _____

Name of Child _____

Ages: _____, _____, _____

Percentages: _____, _____, _____

Name of Child _____

Ages: _____, _____, _____

Percentages: _____, _____, _____

Name of Child _____

Ages: _____, _____, _____

Percentages: _____, _____, _____

Primary Trustee:

Name

_____

Relationship to You _____

Complete Address

_____

_____

Email

_____

Cell/Work Phone

_____

Alternate Trustee:

Name

_____

Relationship to You _____

Complete Address

_____

_____

Email

_____

Cell/Work Phone

_____

Personal Representative:

The Personal Representative is the person(s) whom you wish to ensure that your will is probated and your estate distributed as you desire. This can be one person or two people. Please name a Primary Personal Representative and, if you wish, an Alternate Personal Representative and their relationship to you. Please Note: Unless otherwise specified, your spouse will automatically be named as Primary Personal Representative.

Primary Personal Representative:

Name

_____

Relationship to You _____

Complete Address

_____

_____

Email _____

Cell/Work Phone

_____

Alternate Personal Representative:

Name

_____

Relationship to You _____

Complete Address

_____

_____

Email

_____

Cell/Work Phone_____

Special Bequests

Special bequests are certain heirlooms or specific items you wish to leave to a certain person(s) (example: you want to leave your diamond ring to your granddaughter). Keep in mind that this list should not include the majority of your estate. If there are many items that you wish to give to a specific person(s), you may want to think about doing so ahead of time. Please list any specific bequests, the person to whom it goes, and their relationship to you.

Name

_____

Relationship to You _____

Complete Address

_____

_____

Email

_____

Cell/Work Phone

_____

Item(s) They Are to Receive

_____

Special Bequests Continued

Name

_____

Relationship to You _____

Complete Address

_____

_____

Email

_____

Cell/Work Phone

_____

Item(s) They Are to Receive

_____

_____

Estate Distribution Instructions

If you (and your spouse, if applicable) should die and you have no child(ren) surviving you, between whom would your estate be divided? The following is a list of the most popular methods of disposition:

1. Your grandchild(ren) may inherit their parents' share of the estate.
2. Your grandchild(ren) may inherit equal shares of your estate.
3. If you have no grandchild(ren), you may leave your estate to friends, other relatives, businesses, charities, churches, etc.

Please list how you wish your estate to be disposed in percentages.

If to a business or other organization, be sure to list its complete name and address:

Name of Person

_____

Percent _____ Phone _____

Email _____

Name of Person

_____

Percent _____ Phone _____

Email _____

Name of Person

_____

Percent _____ Phone _____

Email _____

Full Name of Business _____

Percent _____

Complete Address of Business

_____

_____

Business Phone _____

Business Email _____

Full Name of Business _____

Percent _____

Complete Address of Business

_____

_____

Business Phone _____

Business Email _____

Please complete this form as thoroughly as possible. If you need additional space, you can attach additional sheets. If you need additional help, one of our legal secretaries will assist you.

When completed, return to:

Scott A. Rogers, Esq.
Secure Law PC
https://securelawpc.com
2310-A Market Place, Suite A
Huntsville, AL 35801
Phone (256) 513-8282 - FAX (256) 513-8203

Notes

Durable Power of Attorney Information (Optional)

PLEASE USE CAREFUL CONSIDERATION WHEN MAKING YOUR DECISIONS!

A Durable Power of Attorney is the document used to name a person whom you trust to make decisions for yourself or your estate in the event you become unable to do so. Please indicate whether you desire to have a Durable Power of Attorney. If so, list the person you want to name as your Power of Attorney, their relationship to you, and their address.

_____ NO, I DO NOT want a Durable Power of Attorney.

_____ YES, I WANT a Durable Power of Attorney

If You Selected "YES" Above- Please Fill Out the Following Information:

Primary Power of Attorney:

Full Name

_____

Date of Birth _____ Gender _____

Marital Status _____

Complete Address

_____

_____

Email _____

Cell/Work Phone _____

Alternate Power of Attorney:

Full Name

_____

Date of Birth _____ Gender _____

Marital Status _____

Complete Address

_____

_____

Email _____

Cell/Work Phone _____

Your Full Name

_____

Age _____

Date of Birth _____

Complete Address

_____

_____

Cell/Work Phone

_____

Email _____

Spouse Full Name (If applicable)

_____

Age _____ Date of Birth _____

Complete Address

_____

_____

Cell/Work Phone

_____

Email:

_____

Please complete this form as thoroughly as possible. If you need additional space, you can attach additional sheets. If you need additional help, one of our legal secretaries will assist you.

When completed, return to:

Scott A. Rogers, Esq.
Secure Law PC
https://securelawpc.com
2310-A Market Place, Suite A
Huntsville, AL 35801
Phone (256) 513-8282 - FAX (256) 513-8203

Notes

Advance Directive/Living Will Information (Optional)

PLEASE USE CAREFUL CONSIDERATION WHEN MAKING YOUR DECISIONS!

A Living Will is a document that states that in the event that you are declared, by two qualified physicians, to have a terminal condition with no hope of recovery and can only remain alive through the use of life support systems, whether or not you wish your death to be prolonged by the life support systems. If this situation occurs and you do not have a Living Will, your family will make the decision for you. Hospitals generally will ask you or your family, upon arrival, if you have a Living Will.

This is an important decision, so please consider it carefully.

_____ NO, I DO NOT want a Living Will.

_____ YES, I WANT a Living Will

If You Selected "YES" Above, Please Fill Out the Following Information:

Your Full Name

_____

Age _____ Date of Birth_____

Complete Address

_____

_____

Cell/Work Phone

_____

Email

_____

Notes

☐ _____

☐ _____

☐ _____

☐ _____

☐ _____

☐ _____

☐ _____

☐ _____

☐ _____

☐ _____

☐ _____

☐ _____

☐ _____

☐ _____

☐ _____

☐ _____

☐ _____

☐ _____

☐ _____

☐ _____

☐ _____

Primary Health Care Proxy:

_____ I DO NOT want to appoint a health care proxy.

_____ I DO want to appoint a health care proxy. If my attending physician determines that I am no longer able to give directions to my health care providers regarding my medical treatment, I direct my attending physician and other health care providers to follow the instructions of the following:

Full Name

_____

Age _____ Date of Birth _____

Complete Address

_____

Cell/Work Phone_____

Email _____

Alternate Health Care Proxy:

Full Name

_____

Age _____ Date of Birth _____

Complete Address

_____

Cell/Work Phone_____

Email _____

Spouse's Full Name *(if applicable)*

Age _____ Date of Birth _____

Complete Address

_____

_____

Cell/Work Phone

_____

Email _____

Please complete this form as thoroughly as possible. If you need additional space, you can attach additional sheets. If you need additional help, one of our legal secretaries will assist you.

When completed, return to:

Scott A. Rogers, Esq.
Secure Law PC
https://securelawpc.com
2310-A Market Place, Suite A
Huntsville, AL 35801
Phone (256) 513-8282 - FAX (256) 513-8203

CHAPTER 18

Frequently Asked Questions

The following list, which includes the most frequently asked questions regarding a will, is from the law office of Scott A. Rogers – Secure Law in Huntsville, Alabama

1. WHAT DOES "PER STIRPES" MEAN?

"Per Stirpes" is a Latin phrase which means "by representation." In your WILL, it means that if you name a beneficiary in your WILL, for example a child, and that beneficiary dies before you, but leaves descendants, then those descendants will inherit the share your beneficiary would have gotten, but no more than that share.

2. WHAT IS EXECUTION OF A WILL AND WHY IS IT IMPORTANT?

Execution is the procedure whereby your WILL becomes operational. The law of every state requires the signature of the person making the WILL and at least two witnesses in order for the WILL to be considered a legal document. There are some exceptions, but this is the normal method.

3. HOW MANY COPIES OF THE WILL ARE THERE?

When you leave the Attorney's office, you will have the original WILL itself. The attorney's office will keep a copy of your WILL to be retained in your file. If you wish to have copies, Xerox copies are fine, BUT, after you make a copy, write in bold face letters across the front of every page of the copy, the words VOID-COPY. In addition, you should mark through the signature. The reason for all this is that you only want one piece of paper with your signature available for probate, and that is the original. (In Alabama, there is a procedure that if the original WILL is lost; an **executed** copy can be submitted into probate). The copy must be executed at the same time as the original. It is not necessary to file a copy with the

Probate Court, and in most states, it is not permitted.

4. WHERE SHOULD I KEEP MY WILL?

You should keep your WILL in a safe place where your survivors/Personal Representative can easily obtain it. A safe deposit box is okay, but often it is very difficult to open a safe deposit box after death. If you do have one, be sure there are at least two names on the box and that either one can get into the box alone. Another solution would be a safe, or at least a locked strong box, at home; one that is fireproof, or at least fire resistant.

5. CAN I MAKE CHANGES TO MY WILL LATER?

Certainly, but if you do make changes make them on a Xerox copy of your WILL or write them on a separate sheet of paper. Then take the changes and your WILL to your attorney for revision into a new WILL. NEVER WRITE OR MAKE ANY MARKS ON YOUR ORIGINAL WILL. In many states, written marks or changes on a WILL do nothing but revoke your entire WILL.

6. WHAT IS PROBATE?

Probate is a court procedure by which a WILL is proved to be valid, after your death. It is only at this time that your WILL becomes a legal document in full force. Probate is also a term used today to describe the complete process of administration of your estate by the courts and your Personal Representative.

7. WHEN SHOULD I CHANGE MY WILL?

When any of the following occur:

    (1) After a substantial change in the value of your assets;

    (2) Upon the birth or death of a member of your family;

    (3) Upon moving to a different legal residence state or a foreign country;

    (4) When the Personal Representative named in your WILL dies or can no longer be considered competent;

    (5) When a guardian for a minor child must be named or when a new guardian must be appointed;

    (6) When your estate reaches a value level where it is no longer desirable to allow a child

or beneficiary to exercise full control over the share, which he or she will receive after your death;

(7) When you marry, re-marry, divorce, or separate;

(8) When provisions of your WILL no longer apply or need to be changed;

(9) When you acquire additional property of higher value.

Notes

Support

Please contact us at www.probateal.us for real estate services and/or real estate probate consultation. We are here to serve.

Contributors

Law
Scott Rogers, Attorney - Secure Law Firm

Michael Adams, Vice-President - Secure Title

Clergy
Floyd Rodgers, Evangelist – Blue Spring Road Church of Christ

Business
Jerry A Mitchell, President/CEO

Alabama State Black Chamber of Commerce (ASBCC)

Finance
Ken Battles, Founder/President - Compass Urban Stewardship Ministries

Geriatrics
Chanda Crutcher, CEO - American Senior Assistance Programs (ASAP)

Business
Betty Marshall, MBA – Retired City Clerk Treasurer

Review Contributors
Joyce Kimber, Sherica Matthews, Sabrina McClain, Mario Western, Cassidy Wheeler Marvin Williams

MORE INSPIRING BOOKS

These are the links to additional books by Sandra Brazelton and her motivation for becoming a #1 Best-selling Author.

As an engineer, CEO, consultant, and entrepreneur, Sandra Brazelton has always broken down barriers. Therefore, her mission is to help you become your best you!

These books reflect her education in engineering and business, 30 years of experience, leadership, travel, training, and life experiences. Most importantly, based on her faith in God and study of His word, she has cracked the code to personal success.

She has met people from all over the world so she knows that the only race is the human race. She also believes that it is your birthright to succeed and that everything you need for success is already in you.

However, less than 3% of the world's population understand their inherent greatness and the Universal Principles of Wealth. The creative process is to pray, plan, and act. Her goal is to provide real world and relevant solutions to help you succeed. Her prayer is that these books will educate, inspire, and motivate you to unleash your inner warrior and enjoy the blessings of spirituality, health, and wealth that God empowered you to receive.

More Inspiring Books by Sandra Brazelton
sandra@sandrabrazelton.com

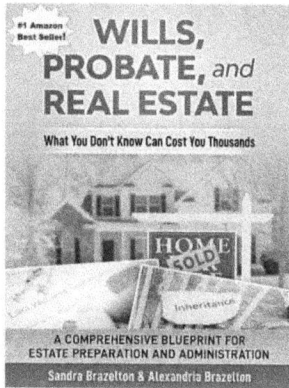

Wills, Probate, and Real Estate
What you don't know can cost you thousands
https://www.amazon.com/dp/1988925312

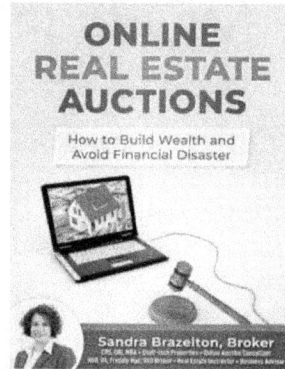

Online Real Estate Auctions
How to Build Wealth and Avoid Financial Disaster
https://www.amazon.com/dp/1796685747

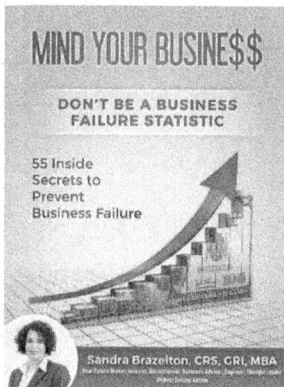

Mind Your Business:
55 Inside Secrets to Prevent Business Failure
https://www.amazon.com/gp/product/1658698827

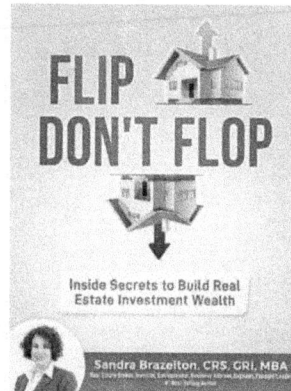

Flip Don't Flop
Inside Secrets to Build Real Estate Investment Wealth
https://www.amazon.com/dp/1736068903

More Inspiring Books by Sandra Brazelton
sandra@sandrabrazelton.com

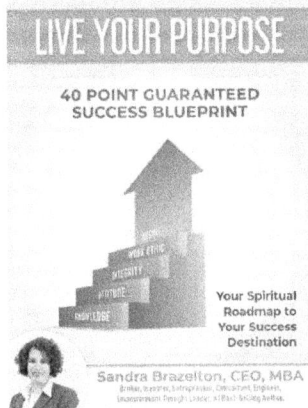

Live Your Purpose
40 Point Guaranteed Success Blueprint:
Your Spiritual Roadmap to Your Success Destination
https://www.amazon.com/dp/1090982755

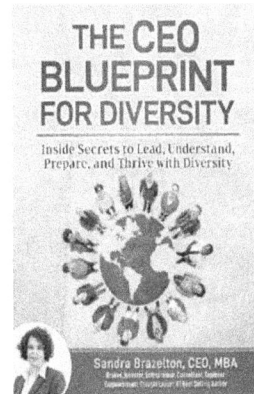

The CEO Blueprint for Diversity:
Inside Secrets to Lead, Understand, Prepare, and Thrive with Diversity
https://www.amazon.com/dp/1736068911

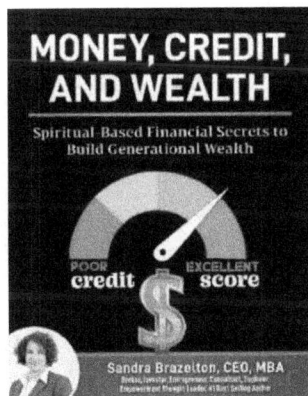

Money, Credit, and Wealth:
Spiritually-Based Financial Secrets to Build Generational Wealth Paperback
https://www.amazon.com/dp/173606890

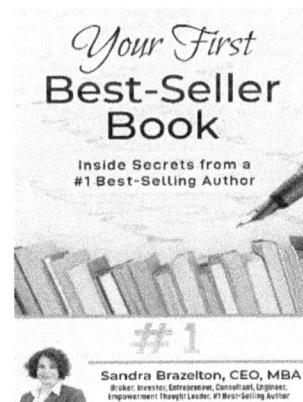

Your First Best-Seller Book
Inside Secrets from a #1 Best-Selling Author
https://www.amazon.com/dp/173606892X

References

AARP - https://www.aarp.org/money/investing/info-2017/half-of-adults-do-not-have-wills.html

https://www.usatoday.com/story/life/people/2018/08/22/legendary-stars-who-died-without-wills-aretha-franklin/83550424/

Legalzoom.com by Heleigh Bostwick
Marketing Communications Specialist

Preparation – Medicaid Liens and Penalties
https://www.finkrosnerershow-levenberg.com/articles/medicaid-basic-rules.html

Skipping out on probate costs By Stan Murray
https://www.investopedia.com/articles/04/121304.asp

About the Author

Sandra and Alexandria Brazelton are real estate brokers with top 1% nationwide credentials.

Together, they have over 30 years of experience as real estate brokers, real estate instructors, online auction consultants, real estate probate advisors, property management specialists, business advisors, listing specialists, and international marketing leaders.

Alexandria Brazelton is a real estate broker, property management specialist, real estate probate advisor, and listing specialist.

<u>Summary of Combined Experience</u>

Real Estate Broker since 1989

Graduate of Leadership Huntsville

Certified Residential Specialist - CRS

Certified Housing Counselor

Certified Debt Counselor

Graduate of the Realtor's Institute - GRI

Real Estate Instructor

Online Auction Consultant

Real Estate Probate Advisor

Property Management Specialist

Experience HUD, VA, REO and Freddie Mac Broker

Business and Personal Success Strategic Consultant and Advisor

Chamber of Commerce – Former Board Member

Member – Huntsville Area Association of Realtors (MLS)

Member – National Association of Real Estate Brokers

Former Engineer for National Missile Defense

Their web site is www.probateal.us

Notes

Legal Release, Disclaimer, and Copyright Protection

While the information contained herein is designed to provide accurate and authoritative information in regard to the subject matter covered, it is offered with the understanding that the presenter(s) are not engaged in rendering legal, accounting, or other professional service. If legal advice or other expert advice is required, the services of a competent professional should be sought. All forms are provided 'AS-IS' without any warranty of any kind, expressed or implied, statutory or otherwise. Any use of information is at the risk of the user.

As stipulated by FTC law, the author makes no guarantees that you will achieve any results from our ideas, models, examples or information provided. This information is the intellectual property of Sandra Brazelton and Alexandria Brazelton

www.ingramcontent.com/pod-product-compliance
Lightning Source LLC
Chambersburg PA
CBHW081504200326
41518CB00015B/2371